D0344957

BACHANALIA

The Essential Listener's Guide to
Bach's *Well-Tempered Clavier*

WITHDRAWN

BACHANALIA

The Essential Listener's Guide to
Bach's *Well-Tempered Clavier*

Eric Lewin Altschuler

Preface by Stephen Jay Gould

Little, Brown and Company

Boston   New York   Toronto   London

First Edition

Library of Congress Cataloging-in-Publication Data
Altschuler, Eric Lewin
    Bachanalia: the essential listener's guide to Bach's Well-tempered clavier / by Eric Lewin Altschuler; preface by Stephen Jay Gould. — 1st ed.
        p.   cm.
    Includes index.
    ISBN 0-316-03529-7
    1. Bach, Johann Sebastian, 1685–1750.   Wohltemperierte Klavier, 1. T.   2. Bach, Johann Sebastian, 1685–1750.   Wohltemperierte Klavier, 2. T.   3. Fugue.   4. Canons, fugues, etc. (Harpsichord) — Analysis, appreciation.   I. Title.   II. Title: Bachanalia.
MT145.B14A5   1994
786'.092 — dc20   93-17817

10   9   8   7   6   5   4   3   2   1

RRD-VA

Published simultaneously in Canada by Little, Brown & Company (Canada) Limited

Printed in the United States of America

*To my mother, Sheila Brody,
and my brother, Randy Altschuler*

ACKNOWLEDGMENTS

THANKS TO: my mother, Sheila Brody; my brother, Randy Altschuler; Dr. Tom Benjamin; The Ford Foundation; Rebecca Merrill; Martha Homer; Professor Stephen Jay Gould; Elizabeth Jacobson-Carroll; Dan Green, the best agent; Jordan Pavlin and Betsy Pitha, the best editors; the Fannie and John Hertz Foundation; Corsillo/Manzone, with art direction by Steve Snider, for the great jacket; Barbara Werden, the best book designer — and Jennifer, Nancy, Ellen, Rob, Rick, Karen, Irene, John, Jon, Joe, Jim, the cashier from Christy's grocery store whose name I have unfortunately forgotten, and all the other people I talked to in stores, in restaurants, at work, or on trains: I got all my good analogies and examples from them.

CONTENTS

**Part Three
The WELL-TEMPERED CLAVIER
Book Two**

Part Four
Appendixes

PREFACE

ODD JUXTAPOSITIONS are the stuff of creativity, and often the key to major intellectual breakthroughs. Darwin developed the theory of natural selection by trying to figure out how Adam Smith's laissez-faire economic system would work in nature; Copernicus and Kepler took aesthetic notions of geometric perfection and applied them to the heavens.

Thus, I did not gag when a young Harvard undergraduate approached me one day and said that he wanted to apply Bill James's style of statistical analysis for baseball teams to the fugues of J. S. Bach's *Well-Tempered Clavier.* Every year, James took each major league baseball team (26 compared with the 48 Bach fugues) and rendered the most daunting pile of technical statistics (several of his own manufacture) into lucid language that any halfway intelligent, even neophyte fan could easily grasp. Moreover, James did this without compromise of intellectual rigor, but only with an uncanny knack for clarity, and for recasting technical concepts in language accessible to ordinary folks. Why not, Eric Altschuler asked me, apply the same conception to Bach's fugues?

The idea struck me at first as nutty, but interesting. If any musical form were accessible to such analysis at all, Bach's fugues would surely be the best candidate. For each is as quirky and as individual as a baseball team, yet all follow the same rules of composition and the same limited set of forms (again like the positions and possibilities of play — enormously varied in outcome, but limited in components to be shuffled and permuted).

Moreover, Eric had a truly remarkable idea, one that I thought might just work. He wanted to make his 48 essays accessible to all serious listeners, even to those without musical training (and unable, even, to read a musical score). Fugues are composed of themes, repetitions, permutations, and supplementary material, all arranged in a definite order (albeit with several things happening simultaneously). A linear description can be written for the form of each fugue. Eric wanted to compose these bare-bones descriptions (called Listener's Guides herein) for each fugue, and then to write a longer essay on some distinctive aspect of the particular piece — just as James gives his basic assessment for each team and then discusses their individualities.

I didn't believe that the scheme would work at first, but I promised to listen to a few attempts. Now, I am a good subject for such a test. I have been a choral singer all my life, but I am no accomplished musician. I can read music adequately (but this skill is not tapped by Eric's method). I play the piano abominably (Eric makes much fun of my limited skill, and I must admit, alas, that he is quite accurate in his derision). I have never played any of the fugues of the *Well-Tempered,* and can barely get through the easiest of the Two-Part Inventions. (Indeed, the only piece I ever mastered in the *Well-Tempered Clavier* is the dead easy Prelude in C Major from Book One). So we tried a few Listener's Guides and, by gum, they work. You have to be willing to listen to the complex fugues more than once, and the going may be a bit slow at first. But after just a few trial runs (of individual fugues, I mean, not of the entire set), the method clicks, and amateurs like myself can hear the form of a fugue for the first time. The effect can be exhilarating.

I then did something that I have never done in twenty years as a Harvard professor. I agreed to serve as an adviser on this project, and to meet with Eric every week during the rest of his undergraduate years. (Harvard professors are not quite so aloof as reputations hold; we really do like students. But, in the craziness of our busy lives in research and writing, we do not make ourselves very accessible either. I had never before even contemplated giving this amount of time, and this degree of attention, to a student project outside my own discipline; indeed, and sad to admit, I have never given nearly this much time to a project within my immediate profession). The result was one of my best educational experiences at Harvard. We met every week for more than two years; we listened to every fugue of the

Well-Tempered Clavier until, Listener's Guide in hand, I could follow the form in detail. The method works. Take it from a dummkopf. No question that I learned much more than Eric during this protracted exercise (though I trust that I taught him a thing or two about writing in return).

This work is an experiment, an exciting innovation in popular education, done in the face of all my initial skepticism. Some rough edges remain, but I am convinced that the basic conception is sound and different. The organization of this book is simplicity itself: some introductory material, and then a "package" for each of the 48 fugues: the "Listener's Guide," followed by a general essay on the fugue, and often a "box" discussing some particular aspect of interest. Please try this book out, and let Eric know what you think. Perhaps we can initiate a hot-stove league with all the passion and fury of its baseball counterpart. But Bach's fugues have no preferred month, and you need no rotisserie league for vicarious enjoyment. This is truly a league for all seasons.

STEPHEN JAY GOULD
Museum of Comparative Zoology
Harvard University

PART ONE

PRELUDE

Introduction

DO DISK jockeys add anything to the music they play?

On the one hand, the answer is an emphatic no. They do nothing more than spin records or put tapes in the cart machine or turn on the compact disk player. How could they add anything?

On the other hand, in three important ways disk jockeys add very much:

1. They tell us about wonderful songs we might otherwise never have heard about.

2. They tell us things about songs we already love so that we enjoy and love them even more.

3. They make connections between and among songs.

I first realized the importance of disk jockeys about 12:42 P.M. one Sunday at Camp Swago, the sleep-away camp I went to for five years. Twelve forty-two P.M. on Sunday, you see, is the time when, for the last twenty years, the radio show "American Top 40" ("AT40") gets toward the end of its countdown and is about to announce the week's number-one song in the land (according to *Billboard* magazine's survey). Counting the hits from coast to coast for all those years and helping "AT40" dominate the 10 A.M.–1 P.M. slot on Sunday was disk jockey Casey Kasem.

At first I was surprised by the large crowds around the radio at 12:42, because the very people who risked getting into trouble by listening to the radio during rest hour had spent the rest of the week saying that "AT40" was stupid and criticizing Kasem's silly stories and corny (probably fake) weekly "long-distance dedications." Come the commercial before the countdown of the top five, you could always find the severest critic closest to the radio telling everyone else to be quiet so he could hear. And once the silly stories were a summer or two old, they were not silly, but important, interesting, and universally known at camp. As for the long-distance dedications, well, let's just say that I heard more than one of them repeated during socials with the girls' camp.

So, the first of the two levels of *The Essential Listener's Guide* is the DISK JOCKEY LEVEL. I am a disk jockey for Bach. Like any disk jockey, I will try to help people to enjoy even more the pieces by Bach they already know and to discover new pieces to love and enjoy.

The second level is the SISKEL AND EBERT LEVEL. Siskel and Ebert, respected newspaper movie critics, are also famous TV movie critics. Their TV show, "Siskel and Ebert," gets "two thumbs up" (as they would say) because there is something appealing about watching a bald man, Gene Siskel, give a movie the "thumbs up" and a fat man, Roger Ebert, give the same movie the "thumbs down," and then watching the two of them argue. Into the Siskel and Ebert level fit the lists and discussions of my Top Ten Fugues, involving the Baseball Hall of Fame and the likes of great Yankee shortstop Phil Rizzuto, my Top Ten Preludes, and other topics.

You may worry that if you don't know what the *Well-Tempered Clavier* is, or what a fugue is, or much about J. S. Bach, you will not be able to understand this book. Do *not* worry! *The Essential Listener's Guide* requires no formal musical training or the ability to read music or prior knowledge about the *Well-Tempered* or Bach. The only requirements for following, understanding, enjoying, and learning from *The Essential Listener's Guide* are a love of listening to Bach or a love of listening to music in general. I discuss only things about the *Well-Tempered* that can be noticed and understood by *listening* to the music. It is not necessary to resort to looking at the musical score.

Why the *Well-Tempered Clavier?* First and foremost, it is a wonderful piece of music, great to listen to and enjoy. But since virtually all of Bach's pieces are wonderful, why have I singled it out? Actually, the *Well-Tempered* is not one long piece but a large collection of short pieces, covering a wide variety of the different styles in Bach's oeuvre. In listening to and studying the *Well-Tempered* we not only have the pleasure of hearing one of Bach's masterworks, we also learn things that can help us enjoy many of his other pieces.

I will explain the structure of the *Well-Tempered* in complete detail later. Here I'll just mention that the pieces in the *Well-Tempered* are divided into pairs. *The Essential Listener's Guide* has a chapter on each pair, which contains:

- A Listener's Guide to the pair. This guide allows the listener to follow the pieces blow by blow.

- An essay about the fugue.

- Now and then a supplementary essay containing additional, sometimes anecdotal, information.

Technical terms are always defined and are printed in SMALL CAPS the first time they are used, or after a long period of disuse.

The Essential Listener's Guide thus requires nothing more than a love of listening to music. So get a recording of the *Well-Tempered Clavier,* begin anywhere, and start listening. I did.

Guide to
Recordings

BACH WAS not only a great composer; he was also the best performer of his day. He needed to be — just to play his own music, especially such difficult pieces as are in the *Well-Tempered Clavier*. In Bach's time there was no more than a tiny handful of performers (if there were any at all) besides Bach capable of playing the entire *Well-Tempered*.

Today the situation is much better. The level of musical performance has risen so much since Bach's time that now numerous performers are capable of giving a superb rendition of the *Well-Tempered*. While I am eager to debate anyone whose Top Ten fugues differ from mine, I have learned that arguing over favorite recordings is far more dangerous territory — into which it is advisable not to tread.

It's hard to go wrong with almost any of the recordings of the *Well-Tempered*. Some of the recordings are listed here. For a complete listing consult the Schwann Opus music catalog.

Recordings of the *Well-Tempered*

Performer	Recording Label
Michel Block	O. M. Records
Edwin Fischer	Angel
Glenn Gould	CBS
Christiane Jaccottet	Intercord
Wanda Landowska	RCA
Gustav Leonhardt	Editio Classica
Davitt Moroney	Harmonia Mundi
Emile Naoumoff	Thésis
Robert Riefling	Simax
Andras Schiff	London
Glenn Wilson	Teldec

What a Life I

TWO WIVES, twenty children. Lüneburg, Arnstadt, Mühlhausen. Brandenburg Concertos, *Well-Tempered Clavier, Saint Matthew Passion,* Mass in B minor. Organist, harpsichordist, violinist, violist, singer. Two hundred cantatas, 350 chorales, six partitas, six English Suites, six French Suites, six cello suites, six sonatas and partitas for solo violin. Directing choirs, directing chamber ensembles, teaching music, teaching Latin. Weimar, Cöthen, Leipzig. Husband, father, musician, composer. Johann Sebastian Bach, 1685–1750. What a life!

Johann Sebastian Bach was born to Johann Ambrosius and Maria Elisabeth Lämmerhirt Bach on March 21, 1685, in Eisenach, Germany, and died on July 28, 1750. In the sixty-five years of his life Bach wrote more than 200 church cantatas, more than 350 chorales, more than 100 chorale preludes, the two volumes of the *Well-Tempered Clavier,* the Brandenburg Concertos, partitas, the English Suites, the French Suites, cello suites, the *Saint Matthew* and *Saint John Passions,* the Mass in B minor, the *Christmas Oratorio,* the *Easter Oratorio,* an *Ascension Oratorio,* the *Goldberg Variations,* the *Musical Offering,* the *Art of the Fugue,* and countless other solo, chamber, vocal, and instrumental pieces.

Bach also had two wives and twenty children, ten of whom lived to adulthood. He taught instrumental and vocal performance, as well as composition and Latin; he prepared two, three, even four choirs for performances; he somehow found time not only to compose well over two hundred hours of music but also to write down the music and copy out parts for all the performers. Just to copy out all of Bach's music would be a life's work for most.

Maria Elisabeth, Bach's mother, died and was buried on May 3, 1694. On February 20, 1695, Johann Ambrosius Bach died. Thus at age of almost ten Bach was an orphan. He went to live with his older brother, Johann Christoph Bach, an organist in Ohrdruf, where Bach learned a lot about organ playing on his own and from his brother.

In 1700 Bach gained a spot in the choir at the Michaelskirche in Lüneburg. Eventually his voice broke, and in 1704 he was appointed organist at Arnstadt, where he stayed until 1707. Bach's earliest composition, *Capriccio sopra la lontananza edel suo fratello dilettissimo (Capriccio on the Departure of His Most Beloved Brother*, BWV 992),* appears to date from the Arnstadt period. Since in Bach's time so few pieces were published and dates of compositions were often not recorded, precise dating for the *Capriccio,* as for many of his pieces, is difficult.

In June 1707 Bach became the organist in Mühlhausen and on October 17 of that year he married his cousin Maria Barbara Bach. Pieces from Bach's time at Mühlhausen include the great Toccata and Fugue in d minor for organ (BWV 565), of horror-movie and *Fantasia* fame, and Cantata 71, *Gott is mein König (God Is My King).*

By the end of 1708 Bach was court organist in Weimar, where he began to blossom and where he remained until 1717. The types of compositions Bach wrote were intimately tied to his duties. In Weimar, Bach mainly wrote organ music, including most of his preludes and fugues for organ, organ trios, chorale preludes, and a collection of organ pieces, *Das Orgelbüchlein (The Little Organ Book).*

In 1717 Bach became music director (*Kapellmeister*) in the court of Prince Leopold of Anhalt-Cöthen. His duties consisted of providing chamber and other instrumental music for Prince Leopold, who was a great music lover and a bit of a musician himself. It was during his tenure in the court of Prince Leopold that tragedy again struck Bach as it had twenty-five years earlier with the death of his parents. Maria Barbara died, while Bach was away, and was buried on July 7, 1720. Some time later Bach married Anna Magdalena Wilcken, on December 3, 1721.

---

*BWV stands for *Bach Werke-Verzeichnis* (Index to Bach's Works), the standard means of numbering Bach's works.

During his years in Cöthen, 1717–1723, Bach wrote many solo, chamber, and orchestral pieces. These include the six suites for unaccompanied cello, six sonatas and partitas for solo violin, concertos in a minor and E Major for one violin, the great D Minor Concerto for Two Violins, and the incomparable Brandenburg Concertos. Bach also wrote many keyboard pieces in Cöthen, some as teaching pieces for his growing family, such as the Six Little Preludes and the Two- and Three-Part Inventions, written for his eldest son by Maria Barbara, Wilhelm Friedemann Bach.

In fact, the *Well-Tempered Clavier* was quite possibly intended as a collection of teaching pieces for Wilhelm. Book One was finished in 1722, when Wilhelm was twelve. Book Two was finished approximately one generation, or twenty years, later, in 1742, when Bach's son John Christoph, by Anna Magdalena, was ten years old — just in time to serve as a teaching piece for his son? Of course, even though only ten of Bach's twenty children lived to maturity, with ten kids one of them was bound to be growing up when Bach was finishing Books One and Two.

On December 11, 1721, Prince Leopold remarried, and his new wife was jealous of all the attention the prince paid to Bach's music. Bach had to move on, and so he applied for the prestigious job of Cantor at the St. Thomas Church and School in Leipzig. The first choice of the town council — Georg Philipp Telemann — did not accept. Neither did the second choice, Christoph Graupner. The council had to settle for its third choice, Johann Sebastian Bach.

In Leipzig Bach wrote an incredible amount of exceptional music, even by his own standards. In each of his first two years in Leipzig — 1723–24 and 1724–25 — he wrote a new cantata every week for the church service. Bach wrote at least three more cantata cycles, large parts of which have unfortunately been lost. All told, over 200 of Bach's cantatas survive. As well, Bach wrote other vocal music in Leipzig, including the *Saint Matthew Passion,* the *Saint John Passion,* the *Magnificat,* the *Christmas Oratorio,* the *Easter Oratorio,* the *Ascension Oratorio,* and the Mass in B Minor. He also wrote a lot of keyboard music in Leipzig, including the French Suites, the English Suites, and the partitas.

Besides composing weekly cantatas, Bach had to prepare choirs to perform at services in four different churches. He had to play the organ for weekly services as well as for festivals and holidays; he had to compose music for weddings and funerals and special occasions; and, in addition, he had to tend to his duties as husband and father. On top of all this Bach had considerable responsibility at the St. Thomas School—instructing the boys in singing, keyboard playing, instrumental music, composition, and even Latin, as well as attending to a host of administrative duties.

In the last decade of his life Bach turned more than ever to complete, comprehensive, contrapuntal collections. These include the *Well-Tempered Clavier* Book Two (1742), the *Goldberg Variations* (1742), the *Musical Offering* (1747), the Canonic Variations on *Vom Himmel hoch* (1747), and the *Art of the Fugue* (1747).

Near the end of his life Bach went blind. Two operations could not save his vision and only weakened his general condition. On July 28, 1750, at the age of sixty-five, J. S. Bach died. But in those sixty-five years he wrote the cantatas, sonatas, partitas; the suites, the chorales; and all the rest. Johann Sebastian Bach, 1685–1750. What a life!

Basic Bach Chronology

March 21, 1685	Johann Sebastian Bach born to Johann Ambrosius Bach and Maria Elisabeth Lämmerhirt Bach	
May 3, 1694	Bach's mother, Maria Elisabeth, is buried	
February 20, 1695	Bach's father, Johann Ambrosius Bach, dies	
1704–1707	Organist in Arnstadt	*Capriccio on the Departure of His Most Beloved Brother* (BWV 992)
1707–1708	Organist in Mühlhausen	Toccata and Fugue in d minor (BWV 565), other organ pieces, Cantata 71
October 17, 1707	Bach marries his cousin Maria Barbara Bach	
1708–1717	Organist in Weimar	*Das Orgelbüchlein,* many other organ pieces

1717–1723	Music Director for Prince Leopold in Cöthen	*Well-Tempered* Book One, Brandenburg Concertos, cello suites, violin concertos, sonatas and partitas for violin, numerous other instrumental and keyboard pieces
July 7, 1720	Maria Barbara dies and is buried	
December 3, 1721	Bach marries Anna Magdalena Wilcken	
1723–1750	Cantor in Leipzig	More than 200 cantatas, passions, masses, chorales, chorale preludes, keyboard music, instrumental music, other vocal music, *Well-Tempered* Book Two, *Goldberg Variations, Musical Offering, Art of the Fugue*
July 28, 1750	Bach dies	

What a Life II

Arnstadt
November 11, 1706
Bach Is Reproved Again

Thereupon ask him [Bach] further by what right he
recently caused the strange maiden to be invited into
the choir loft and let her make music there.
—*The Bach Reader,* p. 53

LET'S LOOK at some events in Bach's life, a few of his writings (in words, not music), and some things that characterize Bach the man. Material in this chapter comes from *The Bach Reader*, a book that includes most of Bach's writings, letters, and documents, as well as accounts of Bach by his contemporaries.*

Hard Work

Bach seems always to have worked hard. Consider his school records, which first appear dating from 1693, when he was eight years old. At Easter in 1693 he was forty-seventh in his class, but in 1694 he was fourteenth. In 1695 he was twenty-third at Easter. In 1694 his mother died and his father in 1695, and he went to live with his brother, so by 1696 he was in a new school.

In July 1696 he was the first among seven new children in his class at the school and fourth overall, and a year later he was first.

---

*The Bach Reader, edited by Hans T. David and Arthur Mendel (New York: W. W. Norton, 1945, revised and with a supplement 1966). The "strange maiden" in the epigraph may have been Bach's cousin and first wife, Maria Barbara.

There are obviously many explanations possible for this increased success at school, but one wonders if perhaps the family tradition — the Bach family, one of musicians for generations, had always worked hard — or even the deaths of his parents stimulated him to do better.

Certainly, Bach never avoided work, and the more the better. Consider the pledge he made when applying for the job of Cantor at the St. Thomas Church and School in Leipzig:

> When I actually enter upon the duties of the said post of cantor . . . I will instruct the boys admitted into the School not only in the regular classes established for that purpose, but also, without special compensation, in private singing lessons. I will also faithfully attend to whatever else is incumbent upon me, and furthermore . . . in case someone should be needed to assist me in the instruction in the Latin language, [I] will faithfully and without ado compensate that person out of my own pocket.
> —*The Bach Reader*, p. 89

Note that he is taking on a lot of teaching responsibilities, including "instruction in the Latin language." And this was obviously not an unfulfilled pre-job pledge. Bach did all these things. So I think it's safe to say that comments like the following, often voiced about Bach: "What a genius that Bach was! He was able to write all that wonderful music even though he had all those children and had to work so hard at his jobs," are misdirected. I call that the IN-SPITE-OF MODEL: Bach was able to write all his music in spite of his other responsibilities.

Here's a different model, the BECAUSE-OF MODEL: it is not in spite of his other responsibilities that Bach wrote such wonderful music but because of them.

It was Bach's job to write music, after all. When he had a job as an organist, he wrote organ music. When he had a job as a chamber musician and chamber-music composer in Cöthen, he wrote a lot of chamber music. When he was cantor of the St. Thomas School in Leipzig and composer of vocal music, Bach wrote most of his vocal music. And he taught, played the organ at four churches and prepared four choirs each week, *and* was a devoted husband and father to growing children.

Indeed, most of Bach's best-known music was written after 1721 — most of the cantatas, oratorios, passions, masses, French

Suites, English Suites, the Italian Concerto, the partitas, the *Well-Tempered Clavier* Books One and Two, the *Musical Offering,* the *Goldberg Variations,* and so on. It's a popular belief that most creative people do their best work when they are very young. (Some composers, to be sure, had no choice: Mozart died when he was thirty-five and Schubert when he was thirty-one.) But Bach probably would never have been able to do so much if he hadn't been working, very hard, since childhood — and, obviously, loving it all.

The psychic income Bach got from all the thousands of concerts and recitals he gave, the church services he played in, the joy his children provided, and the admiration of his students is incalculable. There is nothing better than a piece of work well received by some audience to push us on to our next one. Bach's many responsibilities were a tremendous help to his composing. They say that if you want to get something done, ask the busiest person you know to do it.

Teaching

Besides his devotion to God, the only things more important to Bach than making music were his family and teaching. Bach often intertwined all these by writing pieces to help teach his children music. Many of these, such as the *Well-Tempered,* the Six Little Preludes, and the Two- and Three-Part Inventions, are more than just exercises.

The most famous teaching pieces are the Inventions, composed for Bach's eldest son, Wilhelm Friedemann, around 1723. An INVENTION is a genre of music similar to, but simpler than, a fugue. Bach wrote fifteen Two-Part and fifteen Three-Part Inventions. A glance at the title page of the Two-Part Inventions is fruitful for an insight into Bach's thinking:

UPRIGHT INSTRUCTION

wherein the lovers of the clavier, and especially those desirous of learning, are shown a clear way not alone (1) to learn to play clearly in two voices, but also, after further progress, (2) to deal correctly and well with three *obbligato* parts; furthermore, at the same time not alone to have good *inventiones* [ideas] but to develop the same well, and above all to arrive at a singing style in playing and at the same time to acquire a strong foretaste of composition.

—The Bach Reader, p. 86

Bach's teaching paid off: his sons Wilhelm Friedemann, Carl Philipp Emanuel, and Johann Christoph all went on to become well-known composers.

Number and Word Games

Bach seems to have had a well-developed sense of humor, as well as a fascination for the kinds of games one can play with musical notes and numbers.

For example, from time to time in *The Essential Listener's Guide* we discuss Bach's use of musical codes by which he encrypted his signature in a composition. In old German musical notation, B stood for B-flat and H stood for B-natural, so Bach was able to spell out his name in musical notes: B-flat, A, C, B-natural. As well, in letters: A = 1, B = 2, C = 3, and so on, so that B-A-C-H = 14 and J-S-B-A-C-H = 41 (I and J were the same letter in the German alphabet of Bach's time). We will see Bach doing special things with the fourteenth measure of a piece or the fourteenth entry of a subject in a fugue, or using 14 notes in an interesting way, or marking the forty-first measure, or using the B-flat, A, C, B-natural combination to put his signature on a composition.

We could say, of course, that it wouldn't be hard to find interesting uses of the thirteenth measure or the fifteenth note of a piece, or whatever. Still, it seems very clear that Bach actually put the codes as described in his compositions; scholars and biographers have written many pages analyzing and explaining them.

There is also a wonderful story about a word game Bach played. In May 1747 he visited Frederick the Great, king of Prussia, a musician, a flute player, and a great admirer of Bach. Frederick had written a fugue subject of which he was very proud, and he asked Bach to improvise a fugue on it. Bach improvised a three-part fugue. Then Frederick asked Bach to improvise a six-part fugue on the same theme. Bach demurred, saying a six-part fugue could not be improvised on the spot on any theme. He compromised by improvising a six-part fugue on one of his own themes.

But Bach must have felt bad about not being able to improvise that six-part fugue on the royal theme. In July 1747 he sent Frederick a collection of pieces called *Das musikalische Opfer,* the *Musical Offering.* This wonderful piece includes the three-part fugue improvisation, ten canons, a trio sonata for violin, flute, and continuo, and finally the six-part fugue requested — *all* based on Frederick's royal theme.

Both the three-part and the six-part fugues are written in a style that was old for Bach. To highlight that, Bach called both of them RICERCARS, the name for old-style fugues. And he sent Frederick with the original edition of the *Musical Offering* the following acrostic:

> **R** *egis*
> **I** *ussu*
> **C** *antio*
> **E** *t*
> **R** *eliqua*
> **C** *anonica*
> **A** *rte*
> **R** *esoluta*
> ("At the King's Command,
> the Song and the
> Remainder Resolved
> with Canonic Art")

Life

Finally, we must look at Bach's incredible resilience in the face of the most brutal tragedies. Both his parents died within less than a year of each other. Yet he did increasingly well in school after their deaths. In 1720 Bach's first wife, Maria Barbara, died. Did her death spur him on to his great compositions written after 1720? We'll never know.

Furthermore, only ten of his twenty children survived to adulthood.

There are obviously many explanations for Bach's increased success at school and for his musical achievements, especially in his mature years. Did all these tragedies spur him to do better and to become a great composer? My opinion is that they did, but we will never know.

What Is the WELL–TEMPERED CLAVIER?

THE *WELL-TEMPERED CLAVIER* is a collection of 96 pieces; actually, a collection of 48 pairs divided into two sets of 24, Book One and Book Two. Bach finished Book One in 1722 and Book Two in 1742.

Each pair consists of a prelude and a fugue. As the name implies, a prelude's job is to precede a fugue. Aside from this, there are no rules or restrictions for its composition. The 48 preludes encompass an extremely wide variety of styles.

A fugue must follow a certain set of rules, which serve to provide it with a simple skeleton or structure. Bach fills in that basic structure in so many different ways that the variety of fugues in the *Well-Tempered* is as large as, if not larger than, the variety of preludes. The simple basic structure of a fugue, as well as some subtleties of fugal structure, is explained in the next two essays. Here I discuss the *Well-Tempered Clavier* as a whole.

Learning the meaning of the words *clavier* and *well-tempered* will help us understand what the *Well-Tempered* is, why each book has exactly 24 preludes and fugues, and why the *Well-Tempered* is such a glorious collection.

Instruments

CLAVIER is the German word for "keyboard instrument." Bach put "clavier" in the title to indicate that it was a collection of pieces meant to be played on a keyboard instrument. But which one?

The piano, invented toward the end of Bach's life, is the only keyboard instrument commonly employed today. In Bach's time, the harpsichord was the main keyboard instrument. Even then, however, the question of which instrument to use did not have a simple or a single answer. Along with the harpsichord, the clavichord, pedal harpsichord, organ, and pipe organ were in common use.

I started listening to the *Well-Tempered* in the first place because of different instruments. One day, wandering through the New York Public Library, I saw a record, battered by years of circulation, sticking out of the stacks. It was a recording of Book One by Anthony Newman. Unfortunately, that album, still my favorite recording of Book One, is out of print. The record intrigued me because, among many other instruments, Newman used two or three different kinds of harpsichords, a clavichord, and a pedal organ. Despite some trepidation — I had heard that fugues were too complex to follow without more musical training than I had, rumors I discovered were totally untrue the first time I listened to the record — I decided to borrow it.

The debate today over which instrument the *Well-Tempered* should be played on is just a small part of a larger debate concerning the performance of all Bach's pieces. Should original Baroque instruments be used? Modern instruments? All-male choirs? Women singers? Large orchestras? Smaller chamber orchestras? And on and on.

I once heard a performer say, "The power of Bach's music is that even when played on an empty vacuum tube, it still is wonderful." To that remark I heard another performer respond, "Just because Bach's music sounds good on a vacuum tube doesn't mean we should play it on one." I refuse to get involved in this debate, and will only say that the *Well-Tempered* sounds good when played on any keyboard instrument.

Well-Tempered

WELL-TEMPERED is more difficult to understand than clavier. So first let's talk about chocolate chip cookies. In this world there are three main types: (1) homemade; (2) Mrs. Field's; and (3) Chips Ahoy!

1. Homemade chocolate chip cookies run the gamut from incredibly edible and delicious to completely burned and inedible. In any homemade batch you can find some with lots of chips, some with hardly any, some shaped like perfect ovals, some free forms, some that are too small and some that are too big, some that are so burned

that you wouldn't eat them even if they were the only ones left, some undercooked, and some cooked just right.

2. Mrs. Field's Cookies are more uniform than homemade cookies in terms of size, shape, and amount of cooking (though not in terms of chip distribution). I don't mean to imply that all cookies sold at Mrs. Field's have the same size and shape. If they were all the same, you could buy one cookie without asking for the biggest one in the batch. Mrs. Field's cookies have one other interesting feature: no two Mrs. Field's Cookies stores make cookies exactly the same way.

3. Every Chips Ahoy! cookie is exactly the same size and shape (and has been cooked the same way) as every other Chips Ahoy! cookie, no matter from what bag bought where.

Just as there are three kinds of chocolate chip cookies, there are also three kinds of tuning systems: (1) untempered, (2) well-tempered, and (3) equally tempered.

1. UNTEMPERED is the tuning system used by a bugle, which can play only some notes. These notes, known as HARMONICS, are based on a single FUNDAMENTAL note. Even some of these bugle notes are out of tune. To get them in tune, buglers must use their lips and tongues.

So an untempered scale is like homemade chocolate chip cookies: just as homemade cookies run the gamut from inedible to burned or otherwise disfigured but still edible to amazingly delectable, the notes in an untempered scale run the gamut from unplayable to out of tune to perfectly in tune.

2. In a WELL-TEMPERED tuning system all notes and all keys can be used. Some keys and some notes sound better than others; some keys don't sound very good at all. But unlike those in an untempered tuning system, every note and every key can be used.

A well-tempered tuning system bears a relationship to an untempered tuning system analogous to that of Mrs. Field's Cookies to homemade cookies. A well-tempered tuning system is more uniform than an untempered tuning system, but not completely uniform, just as Mrs. Field's cookies are more uniform than homemade but not completely uniform. Also, just as the cookies bought from one Mrs. Field's Cookies store are slightly different from ones bought at another, the well-tempered tuning system in one part of Germany — Leipzig, for example — would have been different from the well-tempered tuning system used in another part — say, Cöthen or Weimar.

3. In an EQUALLY TEMPERED tuning system all of the keys are the same, just as all Chips Ahoy! chocolate chip cookies are the same. So,

for example, in an equally tempered tuning system, the relationship between the first and sixth note of C Major is the same as the relationship between the first and sixth note of E Major, or the first and sixth note of A-flat Major, or B Major, or G Major, etc. The piano uses an equally tempered tuning system, as have virtually all instruments since the early to middle part of the nineteenth century. Before that, various well-tempered tuning systems were used, the specific tuning system often varying with the time period and the region.*

The Great *Well-Tempered*

Why does each volume of the *Well-Tempered* contain exactly 24 preludes and 24 fugues? If you go to the piano and pick any note as your starting place, C, for example (which is where musicians think the alphabet begins), and then play each note, each white key and black, until you reach the next C, you'll have played exactly 12 different notes.

Since you can have both a major and a minor scale starting on any note, that means there are 12 times two, or 24, different major and minor scales. Each book of the *Well-Tempered* contains one prelude and one fugue in each of the major and minor keys and each book begins with the prelude and fugue in C Major and ends with the prelude and fugue in b minor. Note that capital letters denote preludes and fugues in major keys and lowercase letters the minor keys: thus, the E Major fugue, the c-sharp minor fugue. This typography is followed throughout this book.

Many people believe that the *Well-Tempered* was written by Bach to celebrate the fact that there finally existed a tuning system in which it was possible to use every key. In fact, before Bach's birth there were tuning systems in which that was possible. Others claim that the *Well-Tempered* was written as a celebration of equal tempering; but as equally tempered tuning systems began to come into greater favor only toward the end of Bach's life, he probably never played the *Well-Tempered* on an equally tempered instrument. Besides, he didn't call it the ***Well-Tempered*** *Clavier* for nothing.

The *Well-Tempered* is also said to be an encyclopedic compilation of all the possibilities for fugues, or at least for keyboard fugues.

---

*For a complete discussion of tuning systems see the classic book on the subject, *On the Sensations of Tone as a Physiological Basis for the Theory of Music,* written by the great German physicist Hermann von Helmholtz.

Actually, Bach composed hundreds of other fugues, many of which use compositional schemes nowhere to be found in the *Well-Tempered.* Indeed, for keyboard instruments alone there are at least three other collections — the *Art of the Fugue,* the *Musical Offering,* and the organ fugues — that are themselves said to be encyclopedias of fugal techniques. The big deal about the *Well-Tempered* is that each book, containing one prelude and one fugue in every key, is a wondrous collection of pieces for us to love and enjoy.

What Is a Fugue?

IMAGINE SOMEONE who didn't know much about baseball getting invited to a game that ended in the bottom of the ninth inning when a home run broke a tie score. That person couldn't appreciate the drama of the game-winning blast, not knowing that there are nine innings in a baseball game and that a home run in the bottom of the ninth inning with the score tied will win. Even the slightest knowledge would make the game much more enjoyable.

By learning about fugues, we can enjoy them much more. We will also be able to notice connections among pieces. And although fugues are notorious for their complexity, the truth is they aren't that complicated. The basic structure is as simple as beginning, middle, end. It is this framework, combined with the endless possibilities for filling it in, that makes fugues great to listen to, study, and learn from.

The Historical Development of Fugues

The word FUGUE comes from the Latin *fugo*, meaning "flee," "chase," or "follow." In music the word *follow* often means *imitate*, as it also does in the game Follow the Leader, a game in which we imitate the leader. A fugue was originally a kind of piece in which the various parts followed, or imitated, each other.

An early fugue might have gone something like this: the soprano would start the fugue with a certain melody, then the bass would chase the soprano and come in with the same melody, and the tenor would chase both the soprano and the bass and come in with the same melody. At this point the soprano has probably started on a different melody, and the bass and tenor are preparing to chase the soprano with that second melody also. This chasing, imitating model for a fugue applies to the original fugues, from the fifteenth and sixteenth centuries.

Actually, even the original fugues did not consist entirely of one voice chasing another voice. Besides the CHASING PART, there was always a part of the fugue without chasing that we'll call the OTHER PART. But even with their other parts, these original fugues were relatively short and fit the basic, chasing-and-imitating model.

From the fifteenth century to the time of Bach's birth in 1685, and continuing through to the present, something strange has been happening to all types of musical pieces: they're getting longer and more complicated. Originally, most music pieces were only a minute or two long. But the length of pieces increased so much through the centuries that you practically need to bring a sleeping bag to listen all the way through some of the operas written in the nineteenth century. At the same time, the simple forms of music from the fourteenth and fifteenth centuries have been replaced by much more complex ones.

Fugues did not buck this trend of increasing length and complexity. As they got longer and more complicated from the fifteenth century to 1685, composers had a choice: either expand the chasing part of a fugue or take up the additional space with the other, non-chasing, part. Musicians chose to fill the additional space with the other part, not the chasing part. This was wise: a three-minute piece consisting mostly of parts chasing each other would sound hopelessly complicated and confuse the audience.

So much room began to be taken up by other, nonchasing material that by Bach's time the chasing aspect was almost completely absent from most fugues. No fugue in the *Well-Tempered* shows any substantial signs of its chasing heritage.

Bach's Fugues

We can define a fugue as follows: a piece with three sections — exposition, middle section, coda — that are basically just the beginning, middle, and end.

In the fugue's EXPOSITION, as its name implies, the material is exposed, or introduced. Specifically, in the exposition each voice taking part in the fugue has the theme exactly once.

We call the theme the SUBJECT. When the subject occurs in one of the voices, we say that there is an ENTRY OF THE SUBJECT in that voice. So in the exposition each voice has exactly one entry of the subject. Sometimes, instead of saying that a voice has an entry of the subject, we will say that a voice in a fugue RUNS, or IS RUNNING, an entry.

The exposition of a fugue, with each voice entering in turn with one entry of the subject, is the one aspect of Bach's fugues which still harks back to fugues' chasing heritage.

While an entry of the subject is running in one voice, the other voices have what is known as COUNTERMATERIAL, "counter" as in "against" the subject. Countermaterial that is organized and runs consistently throughout a fugue against the entries of the subject is called the COUNTERSUBJECT. Not all fugues have a countersubject; more than two thirds of those in the *Well-Tempered* do not. There is nothing wrong with, or lacking in, a fugue without a countersubject. For example, the C Major fugue Book One doesn't have one. Some fugues have two and even three countersubjects. For example, c minor Book One and B-flat Major Book One have two.

The ORDER OF ENTRY of voices in the exposition varies greatly, with certain orders of entry strongly preferred by Bach. The most important of these preferences is for the last entry in the exposition of a three-voice fugue to be in the bass: 22 of 26 three-voice fugues have the last entry in their exposition in the bass.

Some fugues have music, known as CODETTAS, between entries of the subject in their exposition. (Codetta has nothing to do with coda, and only an unfortunate historical accident has made these two words so similar.) For a technical musical reason, most fugues that have codettas at all will have one between the second and third entries of the subject; this is especially true for fugues in the *Well-Tempered.*

A fugue's MIDDLE SECTION consists of some kind of alternation between entries of the subject and episodes. An EPISODE is simply anything that isn't the subject. We will discuss different types of episodes a lot in the *Listener's Guide.*

For example, the middle section of C-sharp Major Book One goes entry, episode, entry, episode, entry, episode, entry, entry, episode, episode, episode, entry, entry, entry, episode, entry. Instead of saying that two episodes run in a row, we say that the fugue has one big DOUBLE EPISODE; in this case, instead of saying that three episodes run in a row, we say that the fugue has a TRIPLE EPISODE. So the middle section of the C-sharp Major fugue actually goes entry, episode, entry, episode, entry, episode, entry, entry, TRIPLE EPISODE, entry, entry, entry, etc.

What is the difference between an episode and a codetta? After all, they both serve the purpose of coming in between entries. Here are the most important differences.

1. Codettas, since they come in the exposition — so close to the beginning of a fugue — usually influence the rest of a fugue much more than episodes do.

2. Codettas are usually much shorter than episodes and are usually the same length as or *shorter* than the subject, while episodes are often *longer* than the subject.

3. Codettas, much more than episodes, sound as if they are coming in between entries; episodes sound much more like independent entities.

The last section of a fugue, the CODA, brings the fugue to a close. (Remember, coda has nothing to do with codetta.) The coda begins at the completion of the last entry. Codas have no particular structural requirements.

The Fugue's Structure as a Whole

The longest section of almost all fugues — all but one in the *Well-Tempered* — is the middle section, in general much longer than the exposition and the coda combined. This is somewhat contrary to the usual notion of a beginning, middle, end structure for a story or a movie in which the lengths of the three sections are in closer proportions.

There are fugues in which the middle section isn't the longest. Some of the organ fugues have codas that are longer than their middle section. Some fugues, known as FUGHETTAS, short fugues, have at most only one or two episodes and consist mainly of an exposition. An interesting question is whether the small number of fugues whose longest section isn't the middle one really are fugues at all or a slightly different compositional animal.

The Payoff

The power and beauty of a fugue come from its basic three-section structure: a clear beginning in which all of the voices are introduced without confusion; a manifest division into beginning, middle, end; and a graceful finish with the coda. The potential for different ways to fill in a fugue's basic structure is tremendous: long episodes, short episodes, two entries in a row, three entries in a row, double episodes, triple episodes, and countless permutations and combinations of these. There are also many special devices, such as running the subject in two voices at the same time, or having two subjects for a fugue and not just one, that Bach uses to fill in the middle section. Some of the most common and important of these devices are discussed in the next essay.

Not So Special

NOW THAT we understand the basic structure of a fugue — exposition, middle section, coda — we can examine some of the so-called special devices Bach uses. The most important ones include: STRETTO, having the subject run in more than one voice at the same time; DOUBLE and even TRIPLE FUGUES, fugues with two or even three subjects instead of just one; SEQUENTIAL EPISODES, episodes with sequences in them; and INVERSION, or turning upside down.

Actually, in Bach's fugues special devices aren't that uncommon or special at all. Indeed, more than 40 percent of the fugues in the *Well-Tempered* have stretto in them, more than one in five fugues in the *Well-Tempered* is a double or a triple fugue, and sequential episodes, inversion, and other devices are used extensively throughout the *Well-Tempered*. There is hardly a fugue in the *Well-Tempered* that doesn't have at least one special device. So, far from being musical curiosities meant to be used only on rare and special occasions, special devices are important arrows in Bach's fugal compositional quiver.

Large-Level Special Devices

Let's take a look at some of the most important and common special devices, beginning with those that affect the structure of a fugue on the largest level.

STRETTO is a section of a fugue in which more than one voice is running an entry of the subject at the same time, so that the entries get stacked on top of each other.

People often assume that stretto is usually employed by Bach at the end of a piece to make for a rousing conclusion, with lots of voices coming in on top of each other with the subject. I call this the FILET-MIGNON MODEL: stretto is like filet mignon, a device only to be used on the most unique, rare occasions and when used to take center stage, as filet mignon would be the center of a special meal.

Actually, nothing could be further from the truth than the filet-mignon model. In the *Well-Tempered,* 60 percent of the time Bach starts strettoing in the first half of a fugue. And when Bach does use stretto it is not usually at the center of attention. It is used in conjunction with other devices. So I call this model of stretto the RICE-AND-POTATOES MODEL: stretto is like rice and potatoes, used quite commonly and not as the center of the meal but in conjunction with other parts of the piece or meal.

Another device that influences structure on the large level, often even more profoundly than stretto, is the double fugue or the triple fugue. A DOUBLE FUGUE is a fugue with two subjects. A TRIPLE FUGUE is a fugue with three subjects. Because triple fugues are much more complicated and less common than double fugues (there are only two triple fugues in the *Well-Tempered* compared with eight double fugues), we are going to deal only with double fugues here and discuss triple fugues as they occur.

There are two types of double fugues. In one type, the two subjects have their own expositions and then they combine later in the fugue. F-sharp Major Book One is an example. In the other kind, the two subjects are exposed together. In this second kind, it seems at first that the second subject is just a countersubject that always accompanies the first subject. But the second subject becomes so prominent, often taking over the fugue from the first subject, that we cannot call it a countersubject. An excellent example of this kind of double fugue is f minor Book One.

Smaller-Level Special Devices

Now let's look at some of the devices that affect the structure of a fugue on a smaller level than do stretto and double and triple fugues.

One of the most important, easily heard, and best kinds of episodes is the SEQUENTIAL EPISODE. A SEQUENCE is a musical phrase that contains a smaller musical phrase, a SEQUENCE UNIT, repeated a certain number of times, each time being TRANSPOSED (moved up or down) by the same interval.

INVERSION literally means "turning upside down." There are two types of inversion: MELODIC INVERSION and CONTRAPUNTAL INVERSION. Melodic inversion is discussed briefly here; longer discussions of it and of contrapuntal inversion will be given as the devices occur in the *Well-Tempered*. Melodic inversion means that the melody or a single line is turned upside down. So, for example, if the original line goes up and then down, the melodic inversion of that line will go down and then up. The original line is known as *rectus*, Latin for "right side up." For example, here is the subject of d minor Book One in its rectus ("uninverted") and inverted form.

Rectus

Inverted

Bach uses melodic inversion in two different ways: sometimes he inverts the entire subject, and when such an entry of the subject occurs it is called an ENTRY IN INVERSION. At other times Bach uses only part of the subject (or countersubject, or other thematic material) in inversion.

Bach also uses many other special, or we should make that not so special, devices in the *Well-Tempered*. Some of them include re-expositions, counterexpositions, sequential canonic episodes, double episodes, triple episodes, augmentation, diminution, canons in inversion, and so on. We will discuss these other devices, rarer than the ones we have just talked about, as they occur.

Bach's Big Secret

ONE DAY I was wandering through the record library at the Harvard radio station and saw a CD sticking out. The CD was volume 3 of the organ works of Dietrich Buxtehude. Buxtehude was a great North German organist and composer of organ works who lived from 1637 to 1707 — approximately two generations before Bach. I had read in music history books that Bach learned a lot about organ composition from Buxtehude, but I had heard only a couple of pieces by him and I had never noticed any particular connection between Buxtehude's and Bach's compositions.

One organ fugue listed on the back of the CD cover caught my eye because of its slightly unusual length and key. I listened to the fugue, and to my amazement the subject of Buxtehude's fugue sounded very much like the subject of one Bach's organ fugues. The subjects were not exactly the same, but the similarity was obvious. I listened to the rest of the CD and found three or four other pieces with themes very similar to themes of Bach's pieces (including one from the *Well-Tempered*).

Bach didn't take exact melodies from Buxtehude, but instead one or two ideas, and his resulting themes are almost always much clearer and easier for the audience to follow than Buxtehude's. While there sometimes may be great similarity in their two- or three-measure themes, the working out of those themes in pieces that may run fifty, a hundred, or several hundred measures causes the works of Bach and Buxtehude to be vastly different.

Hearing a piece by Buxtehude with a theme so similar to a theme of Bach's provided a key piece in the puzzle of understanding Bach's Big Secret: How was Bach able to compose over 200 hours of music, almost all of it excellent, and also have the time to copy out parts for the individual musicians, perform on the organ, lead choirs in four different churches, teach singing, teach keyboard playing, teach Latin, and father so many children?

Two hundred hours are just the amount of Bach's music still extant. At least another 50 hours of music Bach wrote down have been lost, and Bach improvised hundreds of other hours of music he never even wrote down. A piece or movement from one of Bach's works rarely is longer than five minutes, and often much shorter. So taking a conservative estimate of 200 hours of music of five-minute pieces and movements, Bach wrote at least 2,400 different movements. In order to compose so many movements, especially with all his other responsibilities, I think Bach must have had a general method for composing pieces and movements so he wouldn't always be reinventing the wheel. I think he used a three-step compositional process:

1. He found or invented an excellent theme.
2. He filled the piece on the small level with the theme and hardly anything else but the theme.
3. He carefully planned the overall structure of the piece.

Step One

After hearing that Buxtehude CD, I started listening to recordings of Buxtehude and others of Bach's predecessors. I found a number of examples of composers' pieces from which Bach seemed to get ideas for his themes. One interesting example is that the subject for the fugue of Bach's Toccata and Fugue in d minor (BWV 565) seems to come from a piece by the German composer Vincenz Lübeck.

In terms of sheer numbers it isn't surprising that Bach used other sources to get ideas for his themes. Anyone would be hard pressed to invent more than 2,000 different excellent themes. So I've started a project to find all the sources for Bach's themes — a Human Genome for Bach project. Anyone interested in getting involved should write to me.

Step Two

Bach organized his music on the small level in a unique way, hardly seen before or since. The magical method Bach used to organize material explains not only why Bach's music is so great, but also why it is harder to get tired of Bach's music than of that by any other composer.

I made up the word MOTIVICNESS to describe the way Bach organized his music. Motivicness means that the motive, or theme, of any piece by Bach is in every measure of that piece, not just in some measures, or in a lot of measures, but in every measure, and also that there is hardly anything else *but* the motive in any measure of any piece by Bach. Of course, I am exaggerating when I say that every measure of every piece by Bach is composed solely of the motive for that piece. But the degree to which Bach utilized the motive of the piece on the small level to the exclusion of other filler material is orders of magnitude greater than that of any other composer.

One easy way to see that all of Bach's pieces are motivic, without even being able to read music, is just to flip through any collection of them. You'll notice that no two pieces look the same. And that's because each piece has a different motive, and each piece uses its motive almost to the exclusion of anything else. This same phenomenon would be observed in a town if everyone in the town were given a pattern different from everyone else's and told to paint his or her house using that pattern and that pattern only. Obviously, no two houses in town would look similar.

Not only does Bach use the motive numerous times in each individual voice, he uses the motive simultaneously in *more than one voice.* Now, most people are able to follow only one moving musical line at once. So most people are not able to follow at the same time two or more lines in Bach's pieces that are moving and using the material from the motive. Thus, our ear makes compromises: first we listen to one line, then another line, then the first, then another, and so on. Each time we hear a piece by Bach we make a different set of compromises, trying (in vain) to keep up with all of the simultaneously moving lines. So each time we hear a piece by Bach we actually hear a slightly different one. Thus we can never get bored with one of Bach's pieces, since we never hear the same version of any one of Bach's pieces twice.

Motivicness is Bach's Big Secret, the secret of his genius.

Step Three

The audience will not like listening to a piece that doesn't have a good overall structure or plan, no matter how good the theme or how cleverly the composer implements the theme in small sections. A piece with an excellent theme and a bad overall structure is like a bad movie with a few good jokes, a boring play with one dramatic scene, or a lousy book with a few nice pages of dialogue.

The necessity for a good overall structure for a musical piece or a book or any other work of art may seem obvious, but it is amazing just how many works of art do not meet that need. Consider the most basic element of a work of art: the length of the complete work. Then consider how many movies or books or pieces of music you know that would have been great if only they had been half their final length. Bach recognized the importance of the overall structure of a piece, and always took the greatest care to see that all of his pieces had a superb and clear overall structure that is easy for the listener to follow.

Guide to the Listener's Guides

WHEN YOU go to a baseball game, you buy a scorecard to help you follow the action. At the theater, you get a playbill for the same reason. When you buy a typewriter or a computer or a stereo, you use the manual to figure out how to set it up and run it. Sporting events also have announcers to give you the play-by-play of the game. The first time you visit a city, you may take a walking or bus tour to learn your way around.

So each fugue in the *Well-Tempered Clavier* has a Listener's Guide to help you follow it. When you listen to a fugue from the *Well-Tempered*, use the Listener's Guide to that fugue. Each Listener's Guide contains a brief sentence about the prelude and various points about the fugue — the number of voices, the major features, and any special devices Bach used.

The main section of each Listener's Guide, called *Form*, sets out, step by step, the structure of the fugue: the entries, episodes, and other landmarks. If you follow the Listener's Guide while listening, you will find it very difficult to get lost. Some of the Listener's Guides contain *Listening Hints* to clear up sections that are difficult to follow.

Occasionally, the entries and episodes come so closely together that there seem to be too many landmarks, which can be confusing. This happens most frequently in fugues with stretto. Stretto, remember, is the name for the section of a fugue in which more than one voice is running an entry at the same time, so the entries get stacked up on top of each other.

   In a Listener's Guide, I indicate that two, or three, or four voices
are running together in stretto by separating mentions of those entries with a *comma* instead of the usual *semicolon* that separates entries that aren't running together. I also explicitly mention the stretto.
Consider, for example, the punctuation in the following section of the
Guide to the C Major Fugue Book One:

> fifth entry in the soprano, sixth entry in the tenor in stretto;
> seventh entry in the alto; eighth entry in the bass, ninth entry
> in the alto in stretto, tenth entry in the tenor in stretto.

This means that the fifth and sixth entries, in the soprano and the
tenor respectively, are running together in stretto. The seventh entry
is in the alto, free from the stretto. Then the eighth, ninth, and tenth
entries, in the bass, alto, and tenor, run in stretto. Notice the commas
separating the fifth and sixth entries and the eighth, ninth, and tenth
entries.

   I also mention when entries are in inversion, augmentation, or
diminution. Usually I mention when entries in a minor fugue are in
major or vice versa.

Tempo Markings in the WELL-TEMPERED CLAVIER

IN THE twentieth century, how do we know how to play music written by Bach in the eighteenth century? We have the scores of Bach's pieces, copied either by Bach, or by one of his wives, children, or students, that tell us which notes to play. But the notes alone don't tell us how fast or with what feeling and spirit to play a piece.

The invention of the metronome around 1820 made the question of how fast to play a piece easy to answer. You've probably seen a metronome, with its pendulum-like rod swinging back and forth, or heard one going "tick, tick, tick." (Recent metronomes are electronic and don't use the pendulum-like rod. Some metronomes now even use a flashing light instead of a tick.) Since the introduction of metronomes, used by musicians for keeping time, composers have been able to specify how fast they want a piece played merely by a METRONOME MARKING.

But metronome markings weren't any help to composers like Bach, of course. And they can't tell musicians with what feeling they should play a piece.

Before the invention of the metronome, composers usually wrote words at the beginning of a piece to indicate its mood and its speed. These words are known as TEMPO MARKINGS, or TEMPOS. Originally, composers used to employ only one or two Italian words as tempo markings. Common tempo markings include ADAGIO (slow), ANDANTE (walking), and ALLEGRO (fast). But since the nineteenth century tempo markings have become more and more elaborate. Composers have also begun to use other languages, such as German and English.

Bach typically used only one or two words to mark the tempo, and often he used none at all, leaving later performers to judge the speed and feeling with which a piece should be played simply from the notes of the piece themselves. In the 96 pieces of the *Well-Tempered* there are only nine tempo markings, of which three are in one piece — the c minor prelude Book One. Only one of the fugues in the *Well-Tempered,* b minor Book One, has a tempo marking. All the tempo markings in the *Well-Tempered* are listed below.

Tempo Markings in the *Well-Tempered Clavier*

Piece	Tempo Marking
BOOK ONE	
c minor prelude	presto (very fast, much faster than allegro)
	adagio
	allegro
e minor prelude	presto
b minor prelude	andante
b minor fugue	largo (very slow, slower than adagio)
BOOK TWO	
C-sharp Major prelude	allegro
g minor prelude	largo
b minor prelude	allegro

Today, concerts by professional musicians are given in specially designed halls, with instruments of uniformly excellent quality using an equally tempered scale. In Bach's time, music was performed in diverse places, such as churches and the courts and studies of nobles, by local musicians, on instruments of varying quality (especially the winds), and using well-tempered scales that varied greatly from town to town. Also, since there were no recordings of music and not much publishing of music, individual pieces were usually not heard by audiences more than once or twice.

The varying performance conditions meant that, of necessity, every time Bach played a piece, it was different from the last time and the next time. He could not be held to a specific performance on a recording. The varying performance conditions, and the lack of uniformity that might be enforced by recordings, contributed to the improvisatory nature of the music of Bach's time, similar to the improvisation in modern jazz and popular music.

So, far from regretting that we don't know exactly the speed with which Bach intended us to play one of his pieces, we can rejoice in knowing that they can be played in so many varied and different ways. Thus, for example, a piece marked allegro sometimes might be played faster, sometimes slower, sometimes happy, and sometimes sad.

PART TWO

The WELL–TEMPERED CLAVIER

BOOK ONE

C Major

BOOK ONE

START STRETTOING directly after the exposition, don't pass Go, don't collect $200.

This is the great STRETTO FUGUE. Twenty-four entries of the one-and-one-half-measure subject are squeezed into this 27-measure fugue, 20 entries into the 19 measures of the middle section. Before the coda there is only a single measure in the fugue that doesn't have at least one entry of the subject, and some measures have as many as two, three, or even four entries.

Though most of us have never tried to write a stretto fugue, it is not hard to imagine how difficult it is to pack so many entries into so few measures. And, of course, just packing the entries in isn't half the job: it's almost like a circus expanding from one ring to three rings. Even if the circus does manage to get enough acts for three rings, without a good ringmaster it will probably turn into a three-ring debacle, because it is too hard for the audience to follow what is happening. And, if the ringmaster isn't careful, the audience could be distracted and miss even the feature acts.

So you might say that a stretto fugue is a little like a three-ring circus, and the composer is the ringmaster trying to make sure the audience stays interested, is able to follow what is going on, and, most important, doesn't miss the main attraction — the subject.

The main compositional problem in writing a stretto fugue is that, as a composer, you lose the use of your main structural landmark. In most fugues that aren't stretto fugues, the exposition is

LISTENER'S GUIDE
to the C Major Fugue
WELL–TEMPERED CLAVIER
Book One

PRELUDE

Very, very motivic. The first 32 (out of 35) measures have identical rhythmic and melodic structures. This massive repetition of rhythm and melodic form (along with the prelude's slow tempo) is the reason it is often assigned to beginning piano students. This prelude is a member of my Top Ten Preludes.

VOICES

4

MAJOR FEATURE AND SPECIAL DEVICE

Stretto. This is the classic stretto fugue.

NOTE

This fugue is one of the more complicated in the *Well-Tempered*. Don't worry! The next fugue, c minor Book One, is a particularly simple one to hear and follow. If the C Major Fugue seems too complicated, then go on to c minor Book One and come back to this fugue later.

FORM

Since there are so many entries coming in on top of one another, it is probably easier to follow the four main sections than the individual entries. There is no stretto in the first section, the exposition; the stretto begins in the second section, intensifies in the first part of the third section, and abates in the second part of the third section, until finally there is no stretto in the fourth section, the coda.

First section, exposition: first entry in the alto; second entry in the soprano; third entry in the tenor; fourth entry in the bass.

Second section: fifth entry in the soprano, sixth entry in the tenor in stretto; seventh entry in the alto; eighth entry in the bass, ninth entry in the alto in stretto, tenth entry in the tenor in stretto.

Third section: eleventh entry in the alto, twelfth entry in the tenor in stretto, thirteenth entry in the bass in stretto, fourteenth entry in the soprano in stretto, fifteenth entry in the soprano in stretto, sixteenth entry in the alto in stretto, seventeenth entry in the tenor in stretto, eighteenth entry in the bass in stretto; nineteenth entry in the tenor, twentieth entry in the alto in stretto, first long-held note in the bass; twenty-first entry in the soprano, second long-held note in the bass, twenty-second entry in the tenor in stretto; one measure without any entries; third long-held note in the bass (held till the end of the fugue), twenty-third entry in the tenor, twenty-fourth and last entry in the alto in stretto.

Fourth section: coda.

LISTENING HINTS

The fifth entry begins very quickly after the end of the fourth entry, so be on your toes. Chords separate the first and second sections, and the second and third sections; listen for them! Listen for the long-held notes in the bass, especially the first and third. The second long-held note in the bass is the hardest to hear.

followed by some sort of alternation between episodes and entries, and the subject is the structural landmark, marking the entries with its presence and marking the episodes with its absence.

But in a stretto fugue, the subject cannot be used as a landmark because it is always present. Obviously, something that is always present functions just as poorly as a landmark as something that is never present. Listening to a stretto fugue is usually like trying to get somewhere you've never gone before, traveling without a map, on roads that don't have any signs.

The wonder of this fugue is not only that Bach was able to get so many entries into so few measures, but also that even with all those entries the audience is still able to follow it. Bach makes it possible, in fact, easy, to follow by being even more fastidious than usual about the clarity of the overall structure of the fugue.

If the sections rather than the subject are the structural landmarks, we have to be able to tell when one section ends and another begins. Bach has been extra careful to make sure that this is completely clear. For example, when the first section ends and the second section begins, there is a chord and then all the voices drop out except the soprano (which has the subject) and the bass. When the second section ends and the third section begins, there is a chord and then all the voices drop out except the alto, which is running the subject. The second part of the third section begins with a long-held note in the bass. Finally, the second part of the third section ends, and the fourth section begins, with the end of the twenty-fourth and last entry of the subject.

The organization of the four main sections is very straightforward. The first section, the exposition, has no stretto at all. The stretto starts in the second section and intensifies in the first part of the third section. It relaxes in the second part of the third section. Finally, in the fourth section of the fugue, the coda, there is neither stretto nor even any entries of the subject at all.

Not only is the fugue organized into sections, but the sections themselves are organized. The six entries in the second section, for example, are arranged in two groups of three entries each. Each group of three entries begins with a pair of entries in stretto followed by a third entry.

The third section is also carefully structured: it has two parts. In the first part of the third section Bach continues the trend in this fugue of intensifying stretto. The first part of the third section has more stretto than any other part of the fugue.

The third section begins with eight entries in stretto with two, three, and once all four voices running the subject simultaneously (entries 15, 16, 17, 18). The eight entries in stretto are followed by a pair of entries (19 and 20) in stretto. However, just at that point the stretto in this fugue begins to abate. Just after the twentieth entry begins there is a long-held, easy-to-hear note in the bass. While the bass is holding a long note it isn't playing any more notes, so it is very easy to hear when the bass isn't playing. So the best way to listen for the long-held note in the bass is to listen for a general absence of any more notes in the bass.

The long-held note in the bass begins the second part of the third section of this fugue. The stretto now abates quite drastically until, finally, in the fourth section, the coda, there is no stretto (or even any entries) at all.

Notice the pair of thirty-second notes (the fifth and sixth notes) in the subject. To me they are the most memorable part of the subject. Bach does the following to make the subject easier for the audience to hear: in the entire fugue (except for the scales in the soprano in the coda, and except for one pair of thirty-seconds in the soprano while the bass has the eighteenth entry) Bach uses thirty-second notes only in this pair in the subject. By being fastidious in not using the thirty-seconds anywhere else but in the subject, Bach has made the subject much easier to pick out.

Bach could have made this a motivic piece by sprinkling the fugue with thirty-second notes. But his use of thirty-second notes only in the subject demonstrates that he does not use motivic material in a trivial way.

A Little More Numerology

There are two numbers that we want to remember for future reference. The first number is 19, or actually, 19/27. Nineteen is the number of the measure in which the first long-held note in the bass occurs. We want to remember that the stretto starts abating in the nineteenth measure of this 27-measure fugue.

The second number to remember is 14. Let's recall the code discussed in "What a Life II." In that code A=1, B=2, C=3, D=4, etc., so that B-A-C-H=14.

There are two 14's to remember as we listen to this fugue: first, the 14 notes in the subject, and second, the fourteenth entry. Of the

24 entries of the subject, 22 run to completion. That's 92 percent! One of the other two entries, the twelfth entry, runs almost all the way to completion. Only the fourteenth entry doesn't run anywhere near to completion.

Bach has entry 14 run only a small piece of the subject rather than the whole thing for an interesting structural reason. If you look at the Listener's Guide you'll notice that both entry 14 and entry 15 are in the soprano, giving the audience the best chance to hear them. It is pretty rare for Bach to run two entries in a row in the same voice, especially when the entries run one after the other with no music between them, as entries 14 and 15 do in this fugue. Note also that entries 14 and 15 run not only during the third section of the fugue, the section of the fugue with the most stretto, but also at the spot in the third section in which the stretto is the most intense. The purpose of the half entry in the soprano, entry 14, and the two entries in a row in the soprano is to give the audience something on which to focus and follow in the section of the fugue in which there is the greatest chance the audience will get confused because of all the stretto.

For more on 14, see "14 + 41 = 141," following f-sharp minor Book One.

Stretto Fugues and Fugues That Use Stretto

There used to be an ad for Snickers candy bars that ran a line similar to the following as a closer: "No matter how you slice it, it comes up peanuts." A STRETTO FUGUE such as C Major Book One, is very much like a Snickers bar. No matter how you slice it, no matter where you look, there are entries in stretto.

We can easily imagine a candy bar or dessert that uses peanuts only in some places: brownies, chocolate chip cookies, or toppings on ice cream sundaes. Just as there are candy bars and desserts that use peanuts only in some places, but certainly not everywhere, there are fugues that use stretto in some places, but not everywhere. The g minor fugue Book One, for example, uses stretto only in the end section, and the E-flat Major fugue Book Two has three pairs of stretto entries distributed through its length. I call those fugues that use stretto only in some places, but not everywhere, FUGUES THAT USE STRETTO.

So there are two classes of fugues that have stretto in them: stretto fugues, which no matter how you slice them come up stretto; and fugues that use stretto, which have stretto in some places but not everywhere. There is a third class of fugues with stretto in them: FUGUES THAT HARDLY USE STRETTO AT ALL. Such a fugue can have at most a single pair of entries in stretto. And even that one pair of entries generally overlaps only at the very end of the subject in the first voice.

FUGUES FROM THE *WELL-TEMPERED* WITH STRETTO

BOOK ONE	BOOK TWO
Stretto Fugues	
C Major	D Major
Fugues That Use Stretto	
d minor	c minor
d-sharp minor	C-sharp Major
F Major	d minor
G Major	E-flat Major
g minor	E Major
a minor	g minor
b-flat minor	b-flat minor
Fugues That Hardly Use Stretto at All	
B Major	d-sharp minor
	f minor
	A-flat Major
Totals 9	11

c minor

BOOK ONE

WHEN YOU come from a city with two teams in all the major sports, as soon as you're old enough to pound on the table, mature enough not to put up with put-downs, well-read enough to invoke the great works on baseball statistics of masters like Bill James, and imprudent enough to make friends with Met fans, you realize the importance of proving that the Yankees — I mean, your team — are the best.

After minimal experience with these pound-on-the-table arguments, you learn that there are two main methods of comparing teams: the sum-of-the-parts method, and the taken-as-a-whole method. Naturally, you choose the one that has your team come out on top.

As its name suggests, the SUM-OF-THE-PARTS METHOD consists of comparing teams player by player and then finding the sum of the individual comparisons to see which team is the best. The TAKEN-AS-A-WHOLE METHOD, on the other hand, consists of comparing teams as a whole, based on the assumption that player-by-player comparisons are not accurate because they do not take into account the intangible factors that don't show up when you go player by player, because the whole of a team is more than just a sum of its parts.

The same two methods can be used to compare fugues. I happen to think that no matter which you use this fugue comes out on top. In order to leave plenty of room for future arguments, though, I am going to weaken my own original claim and simply say that if you use the sum-of-the-parts method for comparisons, c minor Book One is the best fugue in the *Well-Tempered*.

LISTENER'S GUIDE
to the c minor Fugue
WELL-TEMPERED CLAVIER
Book One

PRELUDE

This prelude has four sections. The first section is fast; the second is faster; the third is very slow; the fourth is fast.

Member of my Top Ten Preludes.

VOICES

3

MAJOR FEATURES

Great subject, member of the Top Ten Subjects.

The first episode is a great sequential canonic episode, a member of my Top Ten Episodes, and possibly the best episode in the *Well-Tempered*.

The fourth episode is a great double episode, also in my Top Ten Episodes.

SPECIAL DEVICES

All four episodes are sequential. The first and the fourth episodes are sequential and canonic.

FORM

First entry in the alto; second entry in the soprano; codetta; third entry in the bass; first episode, sequential and canonic (listen for the great move to major); fourth entry in the soprano in major; second episode; fifth entry in the alto in minor; third episode; sixth entry in the soprano; fourth episode (this is a double episode); seventh entry in the bass; coda: extra entry in the soprano.

LISTENING HINT

Beware! The first and second episodes are very short.

All sections of this fugue are very easy to hear and to follow.

The Subject

Great, amazing, wonderful subject, member of the Top Ten Subjects.

The Countersubjects

The second entry of the subject is in the soprano. Against this second entry the alto runs the countersubject. You can hear how well the countersubject complements the subject. Notice especially that the countersubject has fast notes when the subject has slow notes, and slow notes when the subject has fast notes. In general in the *Well-Tempered*, countersubjects are run counter to their subjects in terms of rhythm.

The countersubject in this fugue is very consistent, running against all but two entries of the subject (the first and eighth entries). Countermaterial doesn't need to be *so* consistent for us to call it a countersubject.

This fugue has not one, but two, countersubjects. The second countersubject, containing mainly slow notes, is much more difficult to hear than the first countersubject, despite being just as consistent.

The First Episode

The first episode, the beginning of the first countersubject, is a member of my Top Ten Episodes and is my favorite episode. It is also my favorite single section in the whole *Well-Tempered*.

As you listen to the episode, you'll hear that the sequence unit runs twice and starts to run a third time before breaking off and running into the entry of the subject in major. Bach often runs a sequence unit twice and starts to run it a third time before breaking and running something else: long enough for the sequence unit to become familiar, but not overly familiar, to the audience.

In the sequence unit in the first episode the soprano and alto run in a canon. CANON is basically just a fancy name for a round like "Row, Row, Row Your Boat," where one group starts singing a melody and another comes in a few beats later with the same melody. In this episode the soprano is the LEADER of the canon, and the alto is the FOLLOWER, imitating everything the soprano does two beats later. The bass is FREE FROM THE CANON — that is, the bass does not take part in it. (For more on canons and rounds see "Row, Row, Row Your Boat" at the e minor fugue Book Two.)

Typically, to avoid confusion Bach does not have all the voices in a fugue take part in a canon. Remember how much easier rounds were to sing with only two groups of singers, rather than three or more groups? The combination used in this fugue — canon between the soprano and alto with the bass free — was one of Bach's favorite and best.

Because this episode uses a sequence and a canon I call it a SEQUENTIAL CANONIC EPISODE. Some of Bach's best episodes — six members of my Top Ten Episodes — are sequential canonic episodes.

For this episode Bach builds a sequence unit from the head of the subject and runs the sequence unit — using a canon between the soprano and alto — twice and starts to run the sequence a third time. When the moment arrives that the third run of the sequence unit will break off and do something else, Bach has already arrived in major. The sequence unit, which is just the beginning of the subject, continues on to run the whole subject in major.

The subject of this fugue sounds happy and triumphant in major. I get a chill down my spine every time I hear the sequence in the first episode run once, run twice, and start to run a third time but turn into the subject triumphantly running in major. I never get tired of listening to this episode.

The Fourth Episode

The fourth and last episode in this fugue is what I call a DOUBLE EPISODE. It is double the length and has double the number of different sequences — two compared with one — of the other three episodes in this fugue.

The first sequence of the fourth episode should sound familiar. It is exactly the same as the canonic sequence in the first episode. Remember that when the canonic sequence broke in the first episode, it turned into the subject in major.

Near the end of the fugue Bach wants to stay in minor and not move to major. So when he breaks off the first canonic sequence in the fourth episode he does not move to major, but instead uses a half-measure transition and then starts running a *second* sequence different from the first. Two wonderful sequences in one episode!

If you listen to the end of this fugue, you'll hear that the eighth entry sounds like an extra entry, coming after the main body of the fugue has finished and intended as a way to release the tension built up during the fugue. The long-held note in the bass, the chords in the alto, and the extra voice Bach added for the coda all add to the feeling that the eighth entry functions to release tension.

Let's Take It Outside

Subject in the Top Ten Subjects. Two episodes in the Top Ten Episodes. Great countersubject, great end section. Not a bad part among the other parts in this fugue — the codetta, the other episodes, and so on. Go ahead and try to match this fugue up part for part against another fugue. I love easy arguments.

Sequential Canonic Episodes

At first, all I usually like about a fugue is the subject. I listen to the fugue hoping to hear the subject as much as I can, and I don't really know where in particular it enters during the fugue. But after listening for a while I begin to appreciate the fugue's structure, and instead of hearing the subject wherever it may happen to occur, I notice where the entries fall. Eventually, I begin to notice that there is material between entries of the subject. Finally, I start getting interested in the specific form of the material in the episodes.

Episodes can take many forms. After all, an episode is simply any material that isn't the subject. One of the simplest types of episodes to hear also turns out to be a type with the best sound — the SEQUENTIAL EPISODE.

You'll recall from "Not So Special" that a sequential episode contains a sequence unit that is repeated two, three, or occasionally more times. The simplicity in hearing and following a sequential episode derives from its repetitive material which we become increasingly familiar with during the course of the sequence. In many of his finest sequential episodes, Bach builds the sequence unit from the best material in the subject.

One special kind of sequential episode is a SEQUENTIAL CANONIC EPISODE, a sequential episode that contains a canon. (Remember, a canon is basically just a round.) Several sequential canonic episodes — specifically the first episode in c minor Book One, the fourth episode in F-sharp Major Book Two, and the first episode in C Major Book Two — stand out as some of Bach's most spectacular. In all three, the canon is between the soprano and the alto using material from the HEAD (beginning) of the subject, while the bass does not partake in the canon (or, as we say, the bass has music free from the canon). The canon would get excessively confusing if all the voices took part in it.

The most common arrangements for sequential canonic episodes, and also the best and most easily heard, have the canon between the soprano and alto with the bass free. Our ears, most attuned to the higher ranges, can more easily follow a sequential canonic episode in which the canon is in the upper voices. But not all sequential canonic episodes have the canon between the soprano and the alto with the bass free from the canon. A wide assortment can be found in the *Well-Tempered*, including sequential canonic episodes with the canon between the soprano and the bass, and the alto free from the canon; sequential canonic episodes with the canon between the alto and bass and the soprano free; and many other combinations and permutations.

Bach has sequential canonic episodes that use CANONS IN INVERSION, which is the same as a canon except that the follower does not use the same music as the leader but instead uses the melodic inversion (turned upside down) of the leader's part. The second episode in g minor Book One is a sequential canonic episode that uses a canon in inversion.

Bach even has one sequential canonic episode in which all four voices take part in the canon — the first episode in f-sharp minor Book One. The four voices work in pairs so the canon doesn't get too complicated: the alto and tenor start out simultaneously as the leaders, and two beats later the soprano and bass enter in canon as the followers.

C-sharp Major

BOOK ONE

IMAGINE WE were writing the script for a movie and had decided to structure our movie so that it would end using the same important scene with which it began. So our movie could begin with the first basketball game of the two-game season series between arch-rival high schools and end with the second game of the series.

That's exactly how Bach has structured this fugue: toward its end Bach runs the beginning "scene" of the fugue, the exposition, again. (See the Listener's Guide beginning with entry 9.) I call this special device a reexposition. As its name implies, a REEXPOSITION is just an exact copy of the exposition, a copy that runs any time in a fugue after the exposition.

Let's pause to consider the differences between a reexposition and a counterexposition so that we don't confuse them. A counterexposition is not an exact copy of the exposition, but only similar to the exposition. In both a counterexposition and exposition, all the voices have the subject exactly once, hence the "exposition" part of counterexposition. However, a counterexposition differs from the exposition both in the order of entries of the voices and also in the countermaterial that runs against the entries, hence the "counter" part. A reexposition, on the other hand, is an *exact* copy of the exposition run sometime later in the fugue.

Back to our movie. We've put the rematch game at the end to assure a dramatic ending. The team that lost the first game takes revenge in the second; the star player for one team, an unlikely goat

LISTENER'S GUIDE
to the C-sharp Major Fugue
WELL-TEMPERED CLAVIER
Book One

PRELUDE

Excellent, ultramotivic. A member of my Top Ten Preludes.

VOICES

3

MAJOR FEATURES

Great, triumphant subject, a member of the Top Ten Subjects.

Great return to the subject in the re-exposition following the triple episode.

SPECIAL DEVICES

Reexposition (entries 9–11).

Triple episode (episode 5).

FORM

First entry in the soprano; second entry in the alto; third entry in the bass; first episode; fourth entry in the soprano; second episode; fifth entry in the bass; third episode; sixth entry in the alto; fourth episode; seventh entry in the soprano; eighth entry in the alto;

Fifth episode (a TRIPLE EPISODE): two measures, first sequence runs four times, the sequence has a canon between alto and bass, second sequence runs three times only in soprano and bass, alto has dropped out, long trill in the soprano, third and last sequence still only soprano and bass;

Ninth entry in the soprano, beginning of the reexposition; tenth entry in the alto; eleventh entry in the bass; sixth and last episode; twelfth and last entry in the soprano; coda.

LISTENING HINTS

1. All the episodes are short except the fifth, the triple episode.

2. If you get lost in the triple episode just listen for the long trill in the soprano that comes between the second and the third sequence; you can't miss it.

3. The very beginning of entries 4, 7, 10, and 12 is slightly different from the very beginning of the other entries.

---

in the first game, returns to lead his team to victory in the second; and maybe a substitute player buried at the end of one of the team's benches emerges as the second game's unlikely hero.

However, just a rematch at the end of a movie does not a fantastic finish make. Lots of people don't want to watch even one basketball game, even their own high school team's game, and never mind sticking around for a rematch. Certainly, people from another high school, or another town, even the basketball fanatics, couldn't care less what happens to your high school's team.

So clearly we're going to have to do a lot more work to make sure that our movie has a dramatic end. The first basketball game has to be very exciting if we're going to expect people to stick around for a second game. And we don't just want people tolerating the second game, we want them to be on the edge of their seats practically begging for it. To accomplish this is going to require very careful planning on our part.

With even a very exciting first game, we need to do three things to make a great movie.

First, we need to divide our movie into two nearly equal halves.

Then, in the first half of our movie, following the initial really exciting game, we need to alternate between small portions of more basketball games and nonbasketball scenes, such as the difficulties and successes the players might be having in school, personal and family relationships of the players and coaches, and the relationship of the basketball teams to the rest of their schools and communities. At the beginning of the movie we need to see a bunch of games with plenty of action. If they like the first game, the audience will want to see parts of more games, and, hopefully, they'll become addicted. But we need nonbasketball scenes in our movie so that it's more than the NBA Game of the Week, and alternating between basketball and nonbasketball scenes is one good way to keep the first half of the movie interesting.

Finally, the second half of our movie must begin with a long nonbasketball scene, if our goal is to set up the dramatic second game. By the time the rematch game finally comes around, we want the audience screaming for some basketball.

The plan for our movie should look something like this:

FIRST HALF
1. first game with the arch-rival school   4, 5, 6, etc.
2. nonbasketball scene   nbs bs nbs bs, etc.
3. basketball scene

SECOND HALF
1. long nonbasketball scene
2. second game with the arch-rival school
3. end section

The first half of our movie is made up of a lot of little sections. The second half is made up of only three long sections: the long nonbasketball scene, the second game with the arch-rival high school, and the end section that brings our movie to a close. (The end section connects all the loose ends.)

One last thing about the construction of our movie: in the first half, the wait between basketball games is very short, because the nonbasketball scenes that come in between the games are short. This makes the long nonbasketball scene that begins the second half of the movie seem even longer. It is long already in absolute terms, and now it seems much longer compared with the short wait for the audience between all the other games.

Bach has structured this fugue very much the way we structured our movie. The basketball games in our movie are the entries of the subject in Bach's fugue. The first game with the arch-rival high school (a long stretch of basketball action) in our movie is the exposition in Bach's fugue (a long stretch of entries of the subject). The rematch game in our movie, of course, is the reexposition in our fugue. And the nonbasketball scenes in our movie are the "nonsubject scenes," the episodes in Bach's fugue. Just as we had a long nonbasketball scene in our movie, Bach has a *long* stretch in his fugue without any entries, a long episode, specifically, the triple episode.

Bach's fugue is structured like this:

FIRST HALF
exposition   first episode   fourth entry   second episode
fifth entry   third episode   sixth entry   fourth episode
seventh entry   eighth entry

SECOND HALF
triple episode   reexposition   end section

Just as in the first half of our movie, where we alternated between short basketball and nonbasketball scenes, in the first half of his fugue Bach alternates between individual entries of the subject and short episodes.

Just as the second half of our movie was made up of three long sections, so too is the second half of Bach's fugue. And just as we made the audience wait a long time for the rematch basketball game, Bach makes the triple episode, the long wait between entries of the subject, seem even longer by having the wait between entries in the rest of the fugue very short.

Our goal in constructing our movie was to highlight both the dramatic first game with the arch-rival and the dramatic rematch. Bach's goal in constructing his fugue was to highlight both the dramatic exposition and the dramatic reexposition.

The Just–Looking Method

There are motivic pieces, there are ultramotivic pieces, and then there are the first three preludes, C Major, c minor, and C-sharp Major, from Book One of the *Well-Tempered Clavier*. All three preludes are about as motivic as possible. For example, every measure in the C Major prelude (except the last three) has exactly the same rhythm and extremely similarly shaped lines and chord structures.

You don't even have to listen to these pieces to tell how motivic they are. All you have to do is look. Using what I call the JUST-LOOKING METHOD, even if you can't read music at all, you can learn a tremendous amount about a piece just by looking at its score. As examples, let's consider the first three preludes from Book One.

Take a look at the scores of the three preludes on pages 60, 61, 62. It is clear from just a casual glance that each of the three preludes is using its own motive (structural building block) again, and again, and again in the piece almost to the exclusion of anything else. Also notice how different the three preludes look from each other.

By using the just-looking method we can figure out that the first three preludes from Book One are highly motivic. However, we had discovered that fact before, by just listening. We also could have discovered it by doing a close analysis of the musical score.

But there are things we can discover and learn using the just-looking method that we can't learn when using any other method. Here are the two main ways that we use the just-looking method to discover new and different things.

THE FOREST AND THE TREES

Some Bach pieces are very long and complicated, so that if you analyze every note and detail it's easy to lose the overall structure of the piece. But sometimes, just by looking, it is possible to figure out the overall structure. For example, I figured out that both the c-sharp minor and A Major fugues from Book One are constructed in three sections. I had never noticed this until I used the just-looking method, because I was too caught up in every detail.

CONNECTIONS, CONNECTIONS, CONNECTIONS

Probably the most powerful use of the just-looking method is to notice connections between pieces that we wouldn't otherwise notice, either because we don't have the time or desire to do a more thorough investigation, or because maybe we just hadn't looked for connections. (For example, Brandenburg Concerto lovers might be interested to know that by using the just-looking method I noticed that the first movement of Cantata 54 is very similar to the first movement of the sixth Brandenburg Concerto.)

Prelude 1, C Major

Prelude 2, C Minor

Prelude 3, C-sharp Major

c-sharp minor

BOOK ONE

THIS FUGUE is long, slow, and something else. We'll get to the something else later. At 115 measures this fugue is the second longest in the *Well-Tempered* in terms of measures, and, since it takes about four minutes to perform, it is among the longer third of fugues in the *Well-Tempered* in terms of performance time.

The reason this fugue is so long is that it is a TRIPLE FUGUE. It has three subjects, and Bach needs all 115 measures to expose and develop them. The fugue opens with the exposition of the first subject; the second subject enters in measure 36; the third subject enters in measure 49. The slow pace of this fugue is imposed by the first subject, which consists only of four long and slow notes.

Triple Fugues

It might seem that if fugues with one subject are good, fugues with two or three subjects are better, maybe even two or three times better. However, just as bigger is not always better, and just as too many cooks can spoil the broth, double and triple fugues are not intrinsically — in fact, not usually — any better, grander, or more wonderful than fugues with only one subject.

Fugues with two or three subjects have so much motivic material that they risk becoming too long and complex to follow. Far from being the grandest and most spectacular, Bach's double and triple fugues are typically among the most modest and reserved. They are

LISTENER'S GUIDE
to the c-sharp minor Fugue
WELL–TEMPERED CLAVIER
Book One

PRELUDE

It's nice the way the moving line goes back and forth between the soprano and bass.

VOICES

5: soprano I, soprano II, alto, tenor, bass. This is one of only two five-voice fugues in the *Well-Tempered*. B-flat minor Book One is the other.

MAJOR FEATURE AND SPECIAL DEVICE

Triple fugue.

NOTE

I give the Listener's Guide to this fugue merely for the sake of completeness. This fugue is so long and complicated and has so many entries of the three subjects overlapping that it's almost impossible to follow even with the Guide. Just lean back and try to enjoy it.

FORM

First entry of the first subject in the bass; second entry of the first subject in the tenor; third entry of the first subject in the alto; codetta; fourth entry of the first subject in soprano II; fifth entry of the first subject in soprano I; sixth entry of the first subject in the tenor; seventh entry of the first subject in the tenor; eighth entry of the first subject in the alto; ninth entry of the first subject in the bass; tenth entry of the first subject in the alto;

Eleventh and twelfth entries of the first subject simultaneously in the tenor and bass, *first entry of the second subject* in soprano I in stretto, thirteenth entry of the first subject in soprano II in stretto; second entry of the second subject in the tenor in stretto in inversion; fourteenth entry of the first subject in the soprano II, third entry of the second subject in the bass in stretto; fourth entry of the second subject in soprano I;

Fifteenth entry of the first subject in soprano I, fifth entry of the second subject in soprano II in stretto, *first entry of the third subject* in the alto in stretto; sixteenth entry of the first subject in the tenor, sixth entry of the second subject in the alto in stretto, second entry of the third subject in soprano I in stretto; seventeenth and eighteenth entries of the first subject simultaneously in soprano I and soprano II, seventh entry of the second subject in the alto in stretto, third entry of the third subject in the bass in stretto; fourth entry of the third subject in soprano II, eighth entry of the second subject in soprano I in stretto; nineteenth entry of the first subject in soprano I, ninth entry of the second subject in soprano II in stretto, fifth entry of the third subject in the tenor in stretto; sixth entry of the third subject in the alto, seventh entry of the third subject in the bass in stretto, twentieth entry of the first subject in soprano I in stretto, tenth entry of the second subject in the bass in stretto, eighth entry of the third subject in soprano II in stretto; eleventh entry of the second subject in soprano I, ninth entry of the third subject in the alto in stretto; tenth entry of the third subject in soprano II; twenty-first entry of the first subject in the bass, twelfth entry of the second subject in the alto in stretto, eleventh entry of the third subject in the tenor in stretto; twenty-second entry of the first subject in soprano I, thirteenth entry of the second subject in the bass in stretto, twelfth entry of the third subject in soprano II in stretto; fourteenth entry of the second subject in soprano II, thirteenth entry of the third subject in the bass in stretto; twenty-third entry of the first subject in the tenor, fifteenth entry of the second subject in soprano I in stretto, fourteenth entry of the third subject in the alto in stretto; fifteenth entry of the third subject in the tenor, sixteenth entry of the third subject in soprano II in stretto, twenty-fourth entry of the first subject in the alto in stretto, seventeenth entry of the third subject in the bass; one measure;

Twenty-fifth entry of the first subject in soprano II, eighteenth entry of the third subject in the bass in stretto; sixteenth entry of the second subject in the tenor, nineteenth entry of the third subject in soprano I in stretto, twentieth entry of the third subject in soprano II in stretto; twenty-sixth entry of the first subject in soprano I, twenty-first entry of the third subject in the tenor in stretto, twenty-second entry of the third subject in the alto in stretto, twenty-seventh entry of the first subject in soprano II in stretto, twenty-third entry of the third subject in the tenor in stretto, twenty-fourth entry of the third subject in the alto in stretto, twenty-eighth entry of the first subject in the bass in stretto, twenty-fifth entry of the third subject in soprano II, twenty-sixth entry of the third subject in the tenor in stretto, twenty-seventh entry of the third subject in soprano I in stretto, twenty-eighth entry of the third subject in the bass in stretto; twenty-ninth entry of the third subject in the tenor, thirtieth entry of the third subject in the alto in stretto; thirty-first entry of the third subject in soprano II, thirty-second entry of the third subject in the tenor in stretto; twenty-ninth entry of the first subject in soprano I, thirty-third and thirty-fourth entries of the third subject simultaneously in soprano II and alto in stretto, thirty-fifth entry of the third subject in the tenor in stretto; two and a half measures; thirtieth entry of the first subject in soprano II, thirty-sixth and last entry of the third subject in the alto in stretto.

---

also not very common. Just eight of the 48 fugues in the *Well-Tempered* are double fugues, and triple fugues are even rarer. This is the only triple fugue in Book One, and f-sharp minor is the only triple fugue in Book Two.

Making the Complex Less So

This fugue is on the border of being too complex for the audience to follow, even using the Guide, so I recommend just sitting back and listening to it, rather than trying to follow the 30 entries of the first subject, 16 entries of the second subject, and 36 entries of the third subject — which often overlap, with sometimes as many as four entries of different subjects running at the same time in the five voices.

That this fugue is not hopelessly complex is the result of three factors Bach put into the fugue when planning its structure. The three factors, working from the detail level up through the overall structure of the fugue, are monothematic subjects, separate expositions, and sectional divisions.

A fugue subject can contain just one main idea or many ideas. I call subjects with just one idea MONOTHEMATIC SUBJECTS. Now Bach definitely wanted his fugues — one way or another — to have at least two motivic ideas. Of the 38 single fugues in the *Well-Tempered,* only four have monothematic subjects. The rest have subjects with two, three, or more ideas.

In a double or triple fugue, however, Bach does not need to use a single subject with many ideas to ensure that there's more than one idea. In double and triple fugues Bach can use two or three monothematic but different subjects. Monothematic but different-sounding subjects, easily recognizable and each distinguishable from the others, are also a much needed island of simplicity in a complex double or triple fugue.

In this fugue Bach uses three monothematic but different subjects. The first subject employs all slow whole and half notes and features a jump prominently. The second subject utilizes all fast eighth notes, which move mainly by step. The third subject strikes a middle ground between the first two subjects in terms of rhythm and jumps/steps and uses mostly moderately paced quarter notes, with both a jump and a repeated note.

The three subjects are compared in the chart.

The Three Subjects Compared

	Fast/Slow	*Jumps/Steps*
First Subject	All slow notes	Features a jump
Second Subject	All fast notes	Steps
Third Subject	Moderately paced notes	A jump and repeated notes

The three subjects in this fugue have SEPARATE EXPOSITIONS, beginning in measures 1, 36, and 49 respectively. After their expositions the subjects combine. In the double fugues in the *Well-Tempered* Bach availed himself of different overall structures — exposing the two subjects separately or exposing them together or using many variations on these two basic themes. But in both triple fugues in the *Well-Tempered,* Bach was careful to expose all three subjects separately so that the audience would be able to hear each of them individually.

Finally, even with three utterly monothematic, distinct subjects, exposed separately, a triple fugue can very easily still become a complicated mess once all the subjects have entered. Thus, large-level planning is particularly crucial in a triple fugue. To ensure that it is not completely impossible to follow, Bach has used SECTIONAL DIVISIONS to divide this fugue into three main sections.

The first section starts at the beginning of the piece and continues to the first entry of the fast-moving second subject. Thus the first section of this fugue, dominated by the first subject, is very, very slow. The second section begins with the exposition of the second subject. Like the second subject, the second section uses a lot of fast-moving eighth notes. The second is the longest section of this fugue. The third section goes from measure 95 to the end of the fugue. The third section has no entries of the fast-moving second subject. It uses a lot of slower notes, but is not nearly as slow as the first section.

Dividing this fugue into three sections makes it easier to follow on the large level as it moves from slow notes in the first section, to fast notes in the second section, and back to slower notes in the third and last section.

The Something Else

This fugue is not one of my favorites. I have put this one in my Long, Slow, and Not My Favorite Club.

About Time

The key to figuring out the duration of whole notes, half notes, quarter notes, and other musical notes is called a TIME SIGNATURE, which composers put at the beginning of each piece. A time signature consists of two numbers, one on top of the other, just like a fraction but without the line (e.g., $\frac{4}{4}$ or $\frac{3}{8}$). The top number indicates how many beats there are in each MEASURE, the most elementary structural unit of a piece. The bottom number indicates what kind of note (e.g., quarter note, eighth note, half note) will last for one beat.

So a $\frac{4}{4}$ time signature for a piece tells us that there are four beats in each measure of the piece, and that a quarter note will last for one beat. A $\frac{2}{4}$ time signature indicates that there are two beats in each measure of the piece, and that a quarter note will last for one beat. A $\frac{3}{8}$ time signature says that there are three beats in each measure of the piece, and that an eighth note receives one beat. Other common time signatures include $\frac{6}{8}$, $\frac{2}{2}$, and $\frac{3}{2}$.

By multiplying and dividing by two we can figure out how long notes last. A WHOLE NOTE lasts twice as long as a half note. A HALF NOTE lasts twice as long as a quarter note. A QUARTER NOTE lasts twice as long as an eighth note. An EIGHTH NOTE lasts twice as long as a sixteenth note. A SIXTEENTH NOTE lasts twice as long as a THIRTY-SECOND NOTE. (There are even shorter notes, such as sixty-fourth notes, but since they almost never come up in the *Well-Tempered* we aren't going to worry about them.)

So, in $\frac{4}{4}$ time a quarter note lasts for one beat, a half note lasts for two beats, an eighth note for one-half beat, and so on.

In $\frac{3}{8}$ time an eighth note lasts for one beat, a quarter note for two beats, a sixteenth note for half a beat, and so on.

RESTS AND DOTS

Just as there are whole notes, half notes, quarter notes, and so on, there are also WHOLE-NOTE RESTS, HALF-NOTE RESTS, QUARTER-NOTE RESTS, etc. Each rest lasts as long as the note in its name. For example, in $\frac{4}{4}$ time a whole-note rest lasts four beats, a half-note rest lasts two beats, a quarter-note rest lasts one beat, etc.

Besides the rhythmic values we have discussed already, there are also rhythms known as DOTTED RHYTHMS — for example, DOTTED WHOLE NOTES, DOTTED HALF NOTES, DOTTED QUARTER NOTES, etc. A dot simply adds to a note half its value. So in $\frac{4}{4}$ time, for example, a dotted whole note lasts for six beats, a dotted half note for three beats, a dotted quarter note for one-and-one-half beats, a dotted eighth note for three-quarters of a beat, etc.

What's important about rhythms is not so much the specifics of the different notes and time signatures, but the relative lengths of the various notes: whole notes are longer than half notes are longer than quarter notes are longer than eighth notes are longer than sixteenth notes are longer than thirty-second notes. . . . Also, the lengths of notes are comparable only within the same piece. The tempo of one piece written in $\frac{1}{4}$, for example, could be so slow that an eighth note in that piece is longer than a quarter note in another piece written in $\frac{4}{4}$ with a much faster tempo.

DOUBLE AND TRIPLE METERS

Double and triple meters are slightly more subtle.

In each measure of a musical piece the first beat, known as the STRONG BEAT, is accented more strongly than the others. The third beat of a measure is also accented, though much less strongly than the first beat. The other beats of a measure are known as WEAK BEATS. So, for example, we count $\frac{4}{4}$ time as follows: 1, 2, 3, 4, 1, 2, 3, 4 . . . and $\frac{3}{8}$ time like this: 1, 2, 3, 1, 2, 3 . . .

A DOUBLE METER is a time signature that has two beats or two groups of beats in each measure. One double meter is $\frac{2}{4}$, which has two beats in every measure. Another double meter, the most important one, is $\frac{4}{4}$. This is a double meter since it has two groups of beats—1, 2 and 3, 4—in each measure.

A TRIPLE METER is one with three beats or three groups of beats in a measure. For example, $\frac{3}{8}$ with three beats in each measure is a triple meter. Another triple meter is $\frac{9}{8}$, which has three groups of three beats—1, 2, 3 / 4, 5, 6 / 7, 8, 9—in each measure.

D Major

BOOK ONE

THE MOST interesting thing about this fugue is the last entry: there is none. D Major Book One is one of only two fugues in the *Well-Tempered* that has no last entry. (C Major Book Two is the other.) In the final 11 measures out of a total of 27, there are no entries of the subject at all.

Despite the lack of entries of the subject, the last 11 measures of this fugue don't sound any less like a fugue than the first 16 measures, or than the final measures of a fugue that does have a last entry. Because D Major Book One doesn't stop being a fugue even though there are no more entries after measure 16, we are forced to reconsider, at least a little, our belief that the subject is utterly central to a fugue. That a fugue can sound like a fugue even without any entries of the subject is especially important when considering fugues like the g minor solo violin fugue (the second movement of BWV 1001), and the c minor solo cello fugue (the first movement of BWV 1011), both of which have extended sections without any entries.

You'll notice as you listen to it that this fugue has a shower of fast notes at the head of its subject. The most noticeable thing about the fast notes, of course, is the speed with which performers of this play them. The fast notes, in fact, and also the rest of the subject, can be used as the key to understanding this entire fugue. Before we look at them, though, we are going to do something that is going to seem frighteningly out of place: we're going to talk about horror movies.

LISTENER'S GUIDE
to the D Major Fugue
WELL-TEMPERED CLAVIER
Book One

PRELUDE

Excellent. This prelude has a sound and feeling similar to the next prelude, d minor Book One.

VOICES

4

MAJOR FEATURES

Fast notes in the subject.

The same sequence is used in the second, the third, and fourth episodes.

SPECIAL DEVICE

No last entry.

FORM:

First entry in the bass; second entry in the tenor; codetta; third entry in the alto; fourth entry in the soprano; first episode; fifth entry in the bass; sixth entry in the soprano in minor; second episode, the sequence in this episode runs twice; seventh entry in the soprano; eighth entry in the alto; ninth entry in the soprano; tenth entry in the tenor; eleventh entry in the bass in minor; one measure; third episode, the same as the second episode but in this episode the sequence runs three times; one measure; fourth episode, same as episodes 2 and 3 except in this episode the sequence runs only once; one measure; coda: canon between soprano and bass using the first half of the subject, the bass and soprano run first half of the subject together, all four voices run the second half of the subject, final chords.

LISTENING HINTS

1. The first episode sounds very short, so be sure not to miss it.
2. This fugue has no last entry.

Horror movies have two kinds of scenes juxtaposed: scary scenes and unscary scenes. (During the calm of the unscary scenes I always find myself letting out a breath I must have been holding during a scary scene.) The maximum amount of fright is achieved when a scary scene follows a scene that has lulled us, foolishly, into a state of security. Now back to Bach.

The subject of the D Major Book One fugue clearly has two parts: eight fast notes (thirty-second notes) and then five more notes, two pairs of a long-and-short-note combination (dotted eighth and then a sixteenth) and one more note. Listening to the beginning of this fugue, you'll hear that the subject first goes fast — the eight thirty-second notes — then comes almost to a complete stop, and finally hiccups along in the two pairs of slow-note/fast-note combinations.

In general the subject and the beginning of the fugue itself are very herky-jerky. In contrast the second, third, and fourth episodes are very smooth.

Whenever I listen to this fugue, I feel myself relaxing and letting out a breath when the fugue gets to the second episode (or to the third or fourth). The episodes in this fugue provide a calm section between the herky-jerky sections of the fugue, just as the unscary scenes in a horror movie provide a sense of calm between the scary scenes.

How does Bach manage to end this piece, since, as we know, it has no last entry? In the coda Bach runs the first part of the subject (the eight fast notes) many times, then the second part of the subject (the slow-note/fast-note combination) many times, then the final chords. So even though this fugue has no last entry per se, it has instead a sort of monster-sized "last entry."

d minor

BOOK ONE

AS PEOPLE grow older, my mother always says, they become more and more the way they always have been. If they were mean, they get meaner. If they were sweet, sweeter. If they were stubborn, they get stubborner. In a certain sense, as we will see, Bach's fugues also revert more and more to their old selves as the fugues approach their end.

If you listen to the end of this fugue, the piece appears to end, but instead continues on for six more notes, five plus the final chord. Bach has added extra voices to the fugue for the final six notes. He now uses six voices, as opposed to three voices in the rest of the fugue. In a piece like this fugue, the apparent end is known as the STRUCTURAL END. It is with the structural end that the main structure of the piece ends, and the notes following the structural end (for example, the last six notes in this fugue) seem to come after the end of the fugue.

The best example of a piece with a structural end and notes following it is a hymn that ends with "amen." The structural end is the end of the hymn itself. The notes following the structural end are for the word "a-men," literally coming after the end of the hymn.

The g minor solo violin fugue (BWV 1001, second movement), like our fugue in this essay, d minor Book One, seems to finish, but continues on after its structural end for eight more measures until finally ending. However, the g minor solo violin fugue, instead of adding extra voices after the structural end, subtracts voices.

LISTENER'S GUIDE
to the d minor Fugue
WELL-TEMPERED CLAVIER
Book One

PRELUDE

This prelude sounds like the fifth movement of Cantata 147. (Cantata 147 contains the famous chorale "Jesu, Joy of Man's Desiring.")

VOICES

3

MAJOR FEATURE

Stretto.

SPECIAL DEVICES

Stretto. This is a fugue that uses stretto. There are three groups of two voices in stretto (entries 5, 6; 7, 8; 16, 17) and two groups of three entries in stretto (9–11; 12–14);

Melodic inversion. Entries 6, 10, 11, 12, 14 are the melodic inversion of the subject.

FORM

First entry in the soprano; second entry in the alto; codetta; third entry in the bass; fourth entry in the soprano; first episode; fake entry of the inversion of the subject in the alto; fifth entry in the soprano, sixth entry in the alto in stretto in inversion; one measure; seventh entry in the bass, eighth entry in the alto in stretto; one measure; ninth entry in the bass, tenth entry in the soprano in stretto in inversion, eleventh entry in the bass in stretto in inversion; fake entry of the inversion of the subject in the alto; fake entry of the inversion of the subject in the bass; twelfth entry in the soprano in inversion, thirteenth entry in the alto in stretto, fourteenth entry in the bass in stretto in inversion; second episode; fake entry of the subject in the alto; fifteenth entry in the bass in major; third episode; sixteenth entry in the bass in minor, seventeenth and last entry in the alto in stretto; coda.

LISTENING HINT

If you get lost, here are some places to catch up: the first episode, the ninth entry in the bass, the twelfth entry in the soprano in inversion, the second episode, and the third episode.

Whereas earlier in the violin fugue Bach used two, three, and even four voices at once, after the structural end Bach basically uses only one voice. After the structural end of keyboard fugues, on the other hand, Bach adds more voices than there were in the rest of the fugue.

My mother's wisdom holds for Bach's fugues as well as for people. Keyboard fugues become more keyboardish in the very end section by adding more voices. The violin fugue reduces the number of voices to only a single voice, and becomes more violinish in the very end section. After the structural end each kind of piece reverts to its natural tendency.

Inversions

Like many of the fugues in the *Well-Tempered,* the subject of this fugue is in two parts. The first part consists of a long stepwise ascending scale of eighth notes. The second part consists of one group of four sixteenth notes (fast notes), and then three long notes, the second of which is trilled.

Now it's time to stand on our heads. Not really, but in more than one way, this fugue stands on its head.

In "Not So Special" we said inversion, meaning "turned upside down," comes in two varieties, melodic inversion and contrapuntal inversion. MELODIC INVERSION is when a single line is turned upside down by the composer. If the original version of the line began by heading up and then down, the inverted version of the line heads down then up. CONTRAPUNTAL INVERSION is when the relationship between two parts is turned upside down. If, for example, the bass originally has one thing and the soprano another, when the bass and soprano are contrapuntally inverted, the bass will have what the soprano had and vice versa.

In this fugue Bach uses both melodic and contrapuntal inversion.

He melodically inverts the entire subject, running five entries in inversion, entries 6, 10, 11, 12, and 14. Twice, for entries 9 to 11, and entries 12 to 14, Bach has counterexpositions in which two of the three entries are in inversion. The melodic inversion in this fugue is fairly easy to hear. That's because the subject of this fugue, which begins with a long slow scale ascending upward by step, is a perfect subject to invert melodically. If you can't hear a melodic inversion, try not to listen for all the details of a line but only the rhythm of the line and its overall shape, which is usually the part of a line we can most easily hear anyway. This fugue should demonstrate that melodic inversion is most effective when the line being inverted has a very clear rhythm and overall shape, as does the subject of this fugue.

This fugue's contrapuntal inversion, involving the first and second episodes, is a lot more subtle. Compared with the melodic inversion, it isn't the easiest thing in the world to hear. In the first episode the bass has moving sixteenth notes while the soprano has slow quarter notes. In the second episode the soprano and bass switch — the soprano has moving sixteenth notes and the bass slow quarter notes. The alto does not.

If you listen very carefully, you can hear that the bass part in the second episode is not an exact copy of the soprano part in the first episode, but rather the melodic inversion of the soprano part.

Faked You Out!

In football there is a pass pattern known as the out. There is also a pass pattern known as the out and up. An OUT is a short pattern in which a receiver runs about seven to ten yards down the field and then runs out toward the sideline, where the quarterback throws him the ball. The OUT AND UP, a variation of the out, begins just like an out: the receiver runs seven to ten yards down the field and then runs out toward the sideline. When the receiver is running an out and up, the quarterback doesn't throw the ball to the receiver when he has run out toward the sideline, but only *fakes* throwing the ball. After the fake throw, the receiver takes off up the field and looks for a long pass from the quarterback.

The point of both the out part of an out and up pattern and the fake pass by the quarterback is to try to fool the defensive man covering the receiver into thinking that the receiver is running a short pattern. While the defender is coming up to guard the receiver for the fake short pass, the receiver can get a jump on him and, the receiver hopes, be open for the long bomb from the quarterback. If you use the out and up too often, it won't come as a surprise for the defender, and he will be ready and waiting when the receiver breaks up the field for the long bomb.

Bach's fugues also occasionally use fakeouts, specifically fake entries of the subject. Bach uses part of the subject, and not the whole subject, in such a manner that we actually think that we are going to get a whole entry. In this fugue Bach uses just the first half of the subject, the eighth-note stepwise scale, in RECTUS (uninverted) or inverted form, for his fake entries. There are four fake entries in this fugue, three using the inverted form of the first half of the subject, and one using the rectus form.

Second-Order Motivicness

In this fugue the stretto entries always enter in the same place — after the first half of the subject and the tiniest bit of the second half of the subject. In any (and every) pair of stretto entries or group of three stretto entries, the voices in stretto come in after the first voice has run the first half of the subject, the five eighth notes, and just barely started to run the second half of the subject. This is an example of what I call SECOND-ORDER MOTIVICNESS, or motivicness on top of motivicness: not only is the subject running against itself in stretto (motivicness), but also the entries always come in on top of each other in the same place (second-order motivicness). The true wonder that second-order motivicness demonstrates, especially in Bach's hands, is the number of levels of structure of a piece that the audience is able to hear.

As long as we're talking about motivicness and second-order motivicness: guess where those last six notes after the structural end are taken from? That's right, the first half of the subject. The upper voices have the first half of the subject in melodic inversion, and the lower voices have the first half of the subject uninverted.

E–flat Major

BOOK ONE

GOOD SUBJECT, countersubject, sequential canonic episodes — all the individual parts of this fugue are good. Not great, but good. And taken as a whole? Taken as a whole, this fugue also is pretty good, about twelfth or thirteenth, but not good enough for the Top Ten.

The Subject

The subject begins full steam ahead, next screeches to a halt, then slowly but surely picks up steam again.

The Countersubject

Our main question about the countersubject of a fugue is just how *counter,* how different, it is in comparison to the subject of a fugue. In most fugues of the *Well-Tempered* that have counter-subjects, the countersubject has fast notes while the subject has slow notes and vice versa.

Nowhere is this opposition in terms of rhythm more evident than in this fugue, in which the subject and the countersubject never both have slow notes or fast notes at the same time. The opposition of the subject and the countersubject is the best thing about this fugue.

LISTENER'S GUIDE
to the E-flat Major Fugue
WELL–TEMPERED CLAVIER
Book One

PRELUDE

One of the longest in the *Well-Tempered*, it has three distinct sections: the first section is a free-flowing toccata with a lot of runs; the second section is a chorale; the third section is fugal.

VOICES

3

MAJOR FEATURE

An utterly consistent, but often difficult to hear, countersubject.

SPECIAL DEVICE

A sequence that is used in three episodes: 1, 2, and 6.

FORM

First entry in the soprano; second entry in the alto; codetta; third entry in the bass; first episode; fourth entry in the soprano; second episode; fifth entry in the alto in minor; third episode; sixth entry in the bass in minor; fourth episode; seventh entry in the bass in major; fifth episode; eighth entry in the soprano; sixth episode; ninth and last entry in the alto; coda.

LISTENING HINT

The third episode is very short, and can get lost between the fifth and sixth entries.

The Sequential Canonic Episode

Bach uses the same sequence three times in this fugue, in the first, second, and sixth episodes. The sequence unit runs twice and starts to run a third time before breaking. The sequence is also canonic. All three voices in the sequence, the two taking part in the canon and the one free from the canon, use material from the end of the subject. The noncanonic part uses the material from the subject in AUGMENTATION (longer note values than usual), while the canonic parts use the material from the subject with the same note values as in the subject. The permutations of the various parts for the three occurrences of the sequence are listed here.

The Three-Times-Used Sequence

	First Episode	Second Episode	Sixth Episode
Soprano	Follower	Leader	Noncanonic
Alto	Noncanonic	Follower	Follower (inversion)
Bass	Leader	Noncanonic	Leader

Strict Alternation

In "What Is a Fugue?" we said that the middle section of a fugue consists of some kind of alternation between episodes and entries. One kind of alternation is STRICT ALTERNATION. A fugue that strictly alternates in its middle section never has two (or three or four) entries in a row in its middle section. (Note that even fugues that strictly alternate in their middle section will usually have two entries in a row in their exposition.) So a strictly alternating fugue always has an episode in between any two entries during its middle section.

This fugue strictly alternates during its middle section. Here is a list of such fugues in the *Well-Tempered.*

Fugues That Strictly Alternate in Their Middle Section

Book One	Book Two
c minor	a minor
E-flat Major	b minor
f minor	
F-sharp Major (the first subject)	

A Poor Relation

The subject and the countersubject and its interaction with the subject of this fugue are good, and the three-times-used canonic sequence is first rate. But none of them is good enough to propel this fugue into the Top Ten, which include this fugue's three relatives: c minor Book One, C Major Book Two, and f minor Book Two.

Yes, Bach's love of family extended to pieces in the *Well-Tempered.* To see why I say that this fugue is a member of a family and for more details on its family, look at f minor Book Two. Note that E-flat Major is by far the most distant relative of the family.

E-flat Major Book One shares with its relatives a good, lively, catchy subject and a sequence used in more than one episode, among other characteristics. But the outstanding family trait is an utterly clear distinction between episodes and entries, and of the four fugues in its family, E-flat Major has the *least* clear distinction between episodes and entries. Just listen to c minor Book One, C Major Book Two, or f minor Book Two, and you won't have any problem deciding whether an entry or an episode is running. In this fugue, it can take a second or two to figure out whether an entry or episode is running.

The lack of completely clear, crisp distinctions between episodes and entries, along with a lack of a supremely powerful subject, keep this fugue from joining its relatives in the Top Ten.

Real and Tonal Answers (For Aficionados Only)

Here, and here only, I assume some formal knowledge of music and technical musical language.

In "What Is a Fugue?" I said that in the exposition of a fugue, each voice has the subject exactly once. That was a lie. As we can easily hear, the second voice in a fugue enters a fifth higher than the first voice. "Big deal," you say. "So the second voice comes in a fifth higher than the first voice. Not much of a difference." However, sometimes the second voice doesn't just come in with an exact copy of the subject a fifth higher, but actually with music slightly different from the subject.

The second entry of the subject is known as the ANSWER, since it answers the subject. When the answer is an exact copy of the subject a fifth higher, it is known as a REAL ANSWER. When the answer is different from the subject, it is known as a TONAL ANSWER. Do the differences between a tonal answer and its subject matter? To answer this question we will discuss the various kinds of tonal answers, starting with the simplest type (though not the most common).

MODULATING SUBJECTS AND THEIR ANSWERS

Some subjects MODULATE, or change key. MODULATING SUBJECTS change key from the tonic to the dominant. So, for example, a modulating subject of a fugue in C Major would move from C Major to G Major. If such a fugue had a real answer, it would modulate from G Major to its dominant, D Major. Now our fugue, after only two entries, would have modulated from C Major to D Major. In Bach's time such a modulation was unacceptable. It was thought that a piece, especially at its beginning, should remain close to the key in which it was written. The key of a piece is also known as the piece's TONALITY.

Instead of giving a fugue with a modulating subject a real answer, a composer would use an answer ever so slightly different from the subject of the fugue, in the hope of preserving the tonality of the fugue. Hence the name tonal answer.

A fugue with a modulating subject needs a tonal answer to modulate back to the original key. For our fugue in C Major (whose subject modulated to G Major) the tonal answer must modulate back to C Major. This is accomplished at some point by having the answer go one step lower than the subject. Our fugue whose subject modulated to G Major uses a tonal answer that modulates one step lower than D Major to C Major, instead of giving a real answer that would modulate to D Major. Part of a composer's cleverness is the ability to figure out where in the answer to take the step down, so that the answer sounds both good and not drastically different from the subject.

TONAL ANSWERS THAT DIFFER FROM THEIR SUBJECTS BY ONLY ONE NOTE

In Bach's time, the desire for a piece to remain close to its original key was so great that even the hint of moving away was considered bad. If the subject of a fugue just hinted at modulating, it was deemed necessary to give the fugue a tonal answer.

Fugues that hint at modulation typically emphasize the dominant note. Again using C Major as our example: if we used a subject that hinted of modulating to G Major, it would emphasize the dominant note — G. If we gave such a subject a real answer, then the answer of the fugue, in G Major, would emphasize the dominant note of G Major — D. We would be back to the same problem we had before — the hint of a modulation to D Major. The solution is the same as before: lower the offending note by one step. In our fugue's answer, where a real answer would use a D, the required tonal answer uses a C instead.

Actually, it is not necessary to replace all D's by C's but only those at the most important and easily heard part of the subject, the HEAD (beginning). In fact, usually only a single note at the beginning of the subject needs to be tonally altered in the answer. We call these TONAL ANSWERS THAT DIFFER FROM THEIR SUBJECTS BY ONLY ONE NOTE.

Sometimes a strong dominant note at the beginning of a subject will be repeated two or three times, so that for the answer the same note will have to be tonally altered two or three times. In such fugues, since it is the *same* pitch that must be repeatedly altered, we'll also call these fugues by the same name. Fugues whose tonal answers differ from the subject by one note are by far the most common kinds of fugues with tonal answers. Half of Bach's fugues from the *Well-Tempered* with tonal answers have answers that differ from their subjects by only one note.

OTHER KINDS OF TONAL ANSWERS

Here are four examples of other kinds of tonal answers.

1. Throughout B-flat Major Book One and C Major Book Two, Bach uses PAIRS OF ENTRIES consisting of one entry of the subject and one entry of the subject's tonal answer. In both fugues, the answers differ from their subjects by only one note.

Typically, if a fugue has a subject with an answer differing from the subject by only one note, then the subject makes only a small hint of modulating to the dominant key, so the subject need be balanced by an answer only during the exposition and not throughout the rest of the fugue. However, in certain fugues such as B-flat Major Book One and C Major Book Two, even though the answer differs from the subject by only one note, the subject gives a strong feeling of making a move to the dominant key. Most if not all entries of the subject that hint strongly of a move to the dominant key must be balanced by tonal answers that move back to the tonic key. These fugues have pairs of entries of the subject throughout the fugue, most entries of the subject being immediately followed by an entry of the answer. In fugues with subject/answer pairs of entries the necessity for a tonal answer goes beyond just altering one note in the answer to affecting the entire overall structure of the fugue by forcing the fugue to use pairs of entries and not just single entries.

2. To preserve the tonality of a piece, composers during Bach's time would (1) employ an answer that modulated back to the tonic key for a subject that modulated to the dominant key, and (2) give a tonal answer to strong dominant notes in the subject of a fugue.

There are additional rare and obscure rules for tonal answers. For example, one rule required that a strong leading tone in the subject of a fugue be answered by the sixth degree of the scale in the answer. Fugues in the *Well-Tempered* that TONALLY ALTER A NOTE IN THE SUBJECT OTHER THAN THE DOMINANT include A Major Book One and B Major Book One.

3. The subject of E-flat Major Book One begins with a strong dominant note and also modulates to the dominant key of B-flat Major. The answer for E-flat Major Book One both tonally alters the first note of the subject, and modulates back to E-flat Major. So the subject of E-flat Major Book One is TONAL IN TWO DIFFERENT WAYS and is the only subject in the *Well-Tempered* like that.

4. Interestingly, there are two fugues in the *Well-Tempered* — D Major Book Two and F-sharp Major Book Two — to which Bach gave REAL ANSWERS THAT SHOULD HAVE RECEIVED TONAL ANSWERS, according to the rules. For instance, the subject of D Major Book Two begins with a strong dominant note to which Bach does not give a tonal answer. The interval between the first two notes of the subject of D Major Book Two is a perfect fifth. A tonally altered answer would not have a perfect fifth, but would have a perfect fourth in its place. Bach probably did not tonally alter the answer because he felt that the perfect fifth is so vital that the change caused by a tonal modification of the perfect fifth to a perfect fourth would sap the subject of all its power. In general, in his compositions Bach did not let absolute adherence to rules stand in the way of a good piece.

OVERALL

Approximately one third of the fugues in the *Well-Tempered* have real answers.

Approximately one third have answers that differ from their subject by only one note.

Approximately one third have modulating subjects or other kinds of tonal answers.

So two thirds of the fugues in the *Well-Tempered* have answers exactly the same as their subjects, or answers that differ from their subjects by only one note. Many of the remaining third also have tonal answers with small and difficult-to-hear differences from their subject — for example, one or two notes other than the dominant tonally altered, or a subject that subtly and almost imperceptibly modulates to the dominant and whose answer just as subtly modulates back to the tonic, or a few notes in the subject not tonally altered in the answer. Indeed, there isn't even one fugue in the *Well-Tempered* that has an easily heard tonal answer or a tonal answer that has a large and perceptible effect on the fugue.

TONAL ANSWERS IN BACH'S ORGAN FUGUES

Judging by the *Well-Tempered* alone we would have to conclude that tonal answers, while they exist in abundance, have only slightly more impact on the *Well-Tempered* than a light rain would have on the emperor's new clothes. But the *Well-Tempered* does not exist in a vacuum. Bach wrote hundreds of fugues besides the 48 in the *Well-Tempered*. (See "Organ Fugues" in the Appendixes for more on Bach's organ fugues, and "Other Fugues" for more on Bach's fugues for instruments other than harpsichord and organ.)

It turns out that Bach used fewer tonal answers in his other fugues than in the *Well-Tempered*. For example, approximately half of Bach's organ fugues have real answers, and the remaining half is split almost equally between fugues with tonal answers that differ from their subject by only one note and fugues with other tonal modifications.

Though there are fewer organ fugues with tonal answers than there are in the *Well-Tempered* (50 percent as compared with 67 percent), the tonal answers have a much greater impact on the organ fugues. The reason has to do with the different ways sound is produced on an organ and a harpsichord.

Sound is produced on an organ by air rushing through pipes when the organist presses down the key. Sound is produced on a harpsichord by strings being plucked as the keys are played. Notes can be sustained for a long time on the organ but hardly at all on the harpsichord, and a note dissipates much more quickly on the harpsichord than on the organ. Faster and more intricate rhythms are easier to play on the harpsichord than on the organ, where rhythms are easily obscured by previous notes still holding over. The organ, on the other hand, is very amenable to long and slow notes. So subjects for Bach's organ fugues use much longer and slower notes than do the subjects in the *Well-Tempered*.

A few organ fugues begin with the dominant note repeated a number of times — for example, the G Major Organ Fugue (BWV 541), and the e minor Organ Fugue (BWV 533). The dominant note also is longer and slower than in fugues from the *Well-Tempered*. It is much easier to hear the tonal alteration in these organ fugues than in fugues from the *Well-Tempered* with answers that similarly differ from their subject by only one note.

As organ fugues typically use longer, slower, and grander rhythms than the fugues in the *Well-Tempered*, it is much easier actually to hear and notice a modulating subject and the modulating subject's tonal answer in an organ fugue. Organ fugues with modulating subjects include the C Major Organ Fugue (BWV 547), and the fugue from the Toccata, Adagio, and Fugue in C Major (BWV 564).

Finally, again because they use long and slow notes, organ fugues with real answers that by the rules should have tonal answers are more noticeable. The most famous example of a fugue with a real answer that by the rules should have a tonal answer is the "Little" Fugue in g minor (BWV 578).

In the G Major Organ Fugue (BWV 541), Bach uses the tonal answer to help structure the fugue. Typically in a fugue with a tonal answer, the first entry is the subject in the tonic key, the second entry is the tonal answer in the dominant key, the third entry is the subject in the tonic key, the fourth entry is the tonal answer in the dominant key, and so on if there are more entries in the exposition of the fugue. But for the G Major Organ Fugue (BWV 541) the tonal alteration has such a drastic effect on the power of the subject that Bach decides to use for the fourth entry of the fugue a real answer of the subject (which is the same as the subject) in the dominant key, rather than the tonal answer. Bach considered the answer so strange-sounding that he didn't use any entries of the answer (after the second entry) until near the end of the fugue, when he used the tonal answer in minor, the only minor entry in the fugue, to introduce a fermata.

WHY DO WE NEED CODETTAS?

Finally, let me give the technical reason that a fugue needs a codetta. As we have seen, the second entry in a fugue is in the dominant key. Modulation to the dominant key is the most natural modulation in music and is simply accomplished. However, modulation back from the dominant key to the tonic key is often more difficult. A codetta provides a measure or two for the fugue to modulate back to the tonic key. In the *Well-Tempered,* if a fugue has a codetta we will typically find it between entries 2 and 3 to facilitate the modulation back to the tonic key.

d–sharp minor

BOOK ONE

CONSIDER THREE fugues: this one, a minor Book One, and b-flat minor Book One. All three are long, slow, and use stretto. Though even with their shared characteristics the three fugues are far from identical, they do form a kind of historical progression. From old to new the progression is: b-flat minor Book One, d-sharp minor Book One, and a minor Book One.

B-flat minor Book One is written in a style old for Bach. It is written for five voices, in a $\frac{2}{2}$ time signature, with a highest to lowest order of entries — all features common to fugues before Bach but much less common during and after Bach's time. Also, b-flat minor Book One is dominated by slow, square, and on-the-beat rhythms — common in times preceding Bach's. Even the stretto in b-flat minor Book One, concentrated in a few measures at the end of the fugue, is handled in a measured way indicative of music written before Bach.

This fugue, d-sharp minor Book One, has a more modern feeling than b-flat minor Book One. This fugue is written in $\frac{4}{4}$, the dominant time signature in music since Bach. The subject, while still having somewhat of an old-fashioned spirit, has a more modern selection of faster and varied rhythms and melodic ideas than the subject of b-flat minor Book One.

Stretto pervades this fugue, beginning only 31 percent of the way through and continuing on through the fugue. Bach runs the subject in INVERSION (turned upside down) and in AUGMENTATION (all

LISTENER'S GUIDE
to the d-sharp minor Fugue
WELL-TEMPERED CLAVIER
Book One

PRELUDE

This prelude and fugue are among the longest and slowest pairs in the *Well-Tempered.*

VOICES

3

MAJOR FEATURE

Stretto.

SPECIAL DEVICES

Stretto, inversion, augmentation. This is a fugue that uses stretto.

NOTE

This fugue is so long and complicated and has so much stretto that instead of trying to follow all of the entries, you may just want to sit back and listen.

FORM

First entry in the alto; second entry in the soprano; codetta; third entry in the bass; one measure; fourth entry in the bass; first episode; fifth entry in the soprano; sixth entry in the soprano; seventh entry in the soprano in major, eighth entry in the alto in stretto in major; ninth entry in the soprano in minor in inversion; second episode; tenth entry in the alto in inversion; eleventh entry in the bass in inversion; third episode; twelfth entry in the bass in inversion, thirteenth entry in the soprano in stretto in inversion; fourteenth entry in the alto in inversion; fourth episode; fifteenth entry in the bass, sixteenth entry in the soprano; one measure; seventeenth entry in the soprano; fifth episode; eighteenth entry in the bass in augmentation, nineteenth entry in the soprano in stretto in inversion; twentieth entry in the bass, twenty-first entry in the alto in stretto in major in augmentation, twenty-second entry in the soprano in stretto in major; twenty-third entry in the alto in minor; sixth episode; twenty-fourth entry in the bass, twenty-fifth entry in the alto in stretto, twenty-sixth entry in the soprano in stretto in augmentation, twenty-seventh entry in the alto; coda.

---

the notes twice their usual length), and even with slight ornaments and rhythmic alterations. This is the only fugue in Book One that uses the subject in augmentation, and one of only three fugues in the *Well-Tempered* to do so.

Near the end (entries 24–26) Bach runs a counterexposition in stretto, running the subject in all three practically simultaneously — the augmentation of the subject in the soprano, a rhythmically altered version of the subject in the alto, and an ornamented version of the subject in the bass. The varied use of stretto is one of this fugue's most modern features.

Finally, a minor Book One is the most modern of the three fugues. It is almost future-looking with its moving and jumping subject, its 37 entries, and its end section in which the subject, dramatic chords, and extra voices enter all over the place.

E Major

BOOK ONE

BLOODY HANDS, ten-mile runs, four-hour practices, people throwing up and then passing out. Does this sound like the training regimen for football, wrestling, or maybe a triathlon? Actually, I am describing typical practices for the sport of crew, better known as rowing. Rowing freshman year at Harvard had taught me one thing: the strength workouts we did for football in high school were useless. So over the summer after my freshman year, I resolved to concentrate exclusively on aerobic workouts.

That summer I worked on the kitchen staff at Camp Echo Lake. One of the other guys who worked in the kitchen had wrestled in high school, and he told me that during wrestling practice their coach would make them jump rope for 12 minutes continuously. Now, rowers are supposed to be in better aerobic shape than any other athletes. So I thought, if his wrestling team could jump rope for 12 minutes, I should be able to jump rope for 45 minutes.

I quickly discovered that it was very difficult to jump rope for a specified amount of time if you were watching a clock. It was much easier to jump while listening to a cassette of the appropriate length. Since I loved the *Well-Tempered* and was studying it anyway, and also since most of the preludes and fugues in the *Well-Tempered* are approximately three minutes long, I decided to jump to it. (I had brought the *Well-Tempered* with me to camp on three 90-minute tapes.) That way, I would have a good sense of how long I had jumped, but not so exact as to make me nervous and lose my concentration. At that time my favorite part of the *Well-Tempered* was the

LISTENER'S GUIDE
to the E Major Fugue
WELL-TEMPERED CLAVIER
Book One

beginning of Book One. So I usually jumped to side A of the first tape, which contained the first nine preludes and fugues from Book One of the *Well-Tempered.*

The first 32½ minutes of the tape (C Major through E-flat Major) were wonderful. I used to jump happily along, all the time thinking how much better I was going to be at crew in the fall. But then, but then, came the key of d-sharp minor, and its long, slow, boring, hateful, odious nine-minute prelude and fugue. Do you know how long *nine* minutes are, when you're jumping rope to a slow piece, after already having jumped for 32½ minutes?

But I was tough, damn it. The varsity crew was going to have to look out for me next year. I would hang tough through d-sharp minor. No pain, no gain, right? Easier said than done. But at last my perseverance would be rewarded with the blessed final chord of the d-sharp minor fugue.

Only one more prelude and fugue on the tape, E Major Book One. Only one more prelude and fugue till a rest and a shower. Only one more prelude and fugue till it was time to serve dinner to 500 screaming kids and their counselors.

Oh, E Major Book One, I was always grateful to you for your most salient feature: extreme brevity. This fugue, the shortest in the *Well-Tempered*, takes less than 80 seconds to perform.

This fugue also has the reputation of being UNCOMPLEX, since it doesn't have many special devices like stretto, inversion, augmentation, countersubjects, sequences, or sequential canonic episodes. It is not ULTRA-UNCOMPLEX; the name I give to fugues with no special devices at all. In its third episode a sequence runs twice and starts to run a third time before breaking.

Every fugue by Bach, even this one, has a large number of entries. This fugue (see the Listener's Guide) has 11, below the average number of 12 entries for fugues from the *Well-Tempered*, but still a large number. All fugues in the *Well-Tempered* (with the exception of G Major Book Two, which has six) have at least eight entries of the subject. A fugue is practically destined for disaster without eight or more entries of the subject. This makes a lot of sense: the subject is the most recognizable and important part of any fugue, the star. And thus just as the star is used extensively in a movie, the subject is used often in a fugue.

Preludes I

What about the preludes?

I haven't said much yet about them, and I don't plan to. Far too many trees have given their lives for the sake of inane and insipid discussions focusing on how well a certain prelude/fugue pair from the *Well-Tempered* go together.

This is an example of the FIND-THE-NEEDLE-IN-THE-HAYSTACK THEORY. The find-the-needle-in-the-haystack theory, in this situation, asserts that there is a certain prelude, the needle, out in the haystack of possible preludes that goes perfectly with every fugue. The debate then consists of arguing whether for a certain fugue Bach was able, or unable, to find the perfect prelude for the fugue, to find the needle in the haystack.

The find-the-needle-in-the-haystack theory is not true. It's folly to say that for every fugue there is only one prelude that will run perfectly with it. For every fugue there are many preludes that run well with it, and there are even examples where Bach wrote two or three preludes for the same fugue (for instance, G Major Book Two). This leads to my FIND-THE-HAYSTACK THEORY — for every fugue there are many preludes that will run well with it, haystacks full. All a composer has to do is find the haystack. (From the number of great composers, we can see that just finding the haystack isn't easy.)

More study of the preludes on their own will require a whole other book. Each prelude has its own distinct form that needs individual study: some preludes are dances, others arias, some canonic, others fugal. There are long, short, fast, and slow preludes. And there are further divisions within all of these categories.

I chose this fugue, E Major Book One, for my first essay about preludes because of the special relationship between the E Major fugue and its prelude: the prelude for the E Major fugue, more than any other in the Well-Tempered, really sounds as though it leads into the fugue.

PRELUDE means simply "any piece that comes before another piece." While the form of a prelude can vary widely, and while the relationship of a prelude to its fugue is debatable, the necessity for a prelude is not. A fugue without a prelude sounds too darn short. A prelude provides temporal balance. (Neither the Two-Part nor the Three-Part Inventions have preludes, and in general they sound too short. See the C Major Two-Part Invention Appendix for more on the Inventions.)

I also chose this fugue for an essay because I love this prelude.

It is one of the easiest pieces to play in the Well-Tempered. The simplicity of this prelude's notes mean that even children or beginning piano students can express the power of the motive of this prelude or the subtleties of its ornaments and RALLENTANDOS (slight changes in tempo) with their own feelings.

Notice that virtually the entire prelude uses slow notes — that is, except for one measure, measure 14. Measure 14 uses all faster notes. You can't miss it. (See "14 + 41 = 141" accompanying f-sharp minor Book One for the importance of the number 14.)

I was a little vague earlier when I said that a fugue and a prelude "run well" together. I want to make that more specific now. Preludes and fugues should go together like Spencer Tracy and Katharine Hepburn, Siskel and Ebert, bagels and cream cheese, Bogie and Bacall . . .

e minor

BOOK ONE

THERE USED to be a TV show called "Eight Is Enough." The show starred Dick Van Patten as Tom Bradford, a columnist and recent widower, trying to deal with eight children from his first marriage, a new wife, and life in California in general. The point of "Eight Is Enough" was that with the eight kids, Dad, and new wife Abby working together, things generally managed (barely) to come out all right in the end. But a ninth Bradford child? Forget it!

While the Bradfords pushed the *upper* limit on the number of children in a family, this fugue, the only two-voice fugue in the *Well-Tempered,* pushes the *lower* limit on the number of voices in a fugue. Are two voices enough for a fugue?

Many of the techniques and devices so common in three- and four-voice fugues cannot be used in a two-voice fugue. Typically, in three- or four-voice fugues, to get some textual variety Bach will have one of the voices drop out for a few measures. But in a two-voice fugue the fugue would then become a solo and sound a bit silly. Or consider such special devices as three voices running in stretto at the same time, or two voices running in stretto while a third voice has the countersubject. These devices, of course, are not available at all in a two-voice fugue.

Writing a fugue with only two voices is sort of like trying to fight with one hand tied behind your back. Nonetheless, considering all the usual fugal techniques not available for use in a two-voice fugue, e minor Book One is a good one.

LISTENER'S GUIDE
to the e minor Fugue
WELL-TEMPERED CLAVIER
Book One

PRELUDE

The first half of this prelude goes at a fast pace, and the second half goes even faster (Bach has marked the second half "presto," "very, very fast"). See "Tempo Markings" for more.

VOICES

2

MAJOR FEATURE

The only two-voice fugue in the *Well-Tempered*.

SPECIAL DEVICES

Chromatic subject.

Sequential episodes (all four episodes).

Sequential canonic episodes (episodes 2 and 4).

Consistent countersubject. The countersubject in this fugue accompanies all entries of the subject except the first and last entries.

Paired entries.

FORM

First entry in the soprano; second entry in the bass; first episode; third entry in the soprano; fourth entry in the bass; second episode; fifth entry in the bass; sixth entry in the soprano; third episode; seventh entry in the bass; eighth entry in the soprano; fourth episode; ninth entry in the soprano; tenth entry in the bass; coda.

LISTENING HINTS

1. The first and the third episodes and the second and the fourth episodes are almost the same. The only difference is that the soprano and the bass contrapuntally invert their parts.

2. The ninth and tenth entries are not full entries: they use only the first half of the subject.

It is amazing that Bach was able to write such a good fugue with only two voices. To do so, since the available techniques are limited, Bach sometimes can only hint, by shadows and feints, at sounds familiar to us from three- and four-voice fugues. The main technique Bach employs is to bombard our ears with special devices, and hope that we forget the fugue has only two voices.

When we hear a special device, such as a sequential canonic episode, we focus on that device and pretty much forget that only two voices are performing it. Some of the many special devices used in this fugue are:

Chromatic subject. The subject of this fugue uses a lot of CHROMATIC NOTES (notes borrowed from another key). It is uncommon for a fugue to have chromatic notes in its subject.

Sequential episodes. All four episodes in this fugue are sequential.

Sequential canonic episodes. The second and fourth episodes are sequential and canonic.

The same sequence used in more than one episode. Bach uses the same sequence in the first and third episodes and the second and fourth episodes. The only difference between the first and third, and second and fourth, episodes is that the parts are CONTRAPUNTALLY INVERTED (turned upside down). In the third episode the soprano has what the bass had in the first episode, and the bass has what the soprano has. The same goes for the second and fourth episodes.

Consistent countersubject. This fugue has a consistent countersubject that runs against all the entries in the fugue except the last and the first.

Paired entries. All the entries in this fugue come in pairs. So this fugue is filled with counterexpositions and reexpositions.

There are even some one-voice fugues Bach wrote for solo violin (BWV 1001) and cello (BWV 1011). In these fugues, Bach has to be even more clever than in this fugue in using hints and devices to remind the audience of a fugue with a full complement of three, four, or more voices. For example, consider that even the absolutely crucial feature in a fugue of the subject entering in one voice and then another voice can only be hinted at in a solo fugue.

Two voices. It's more than enough for Bach.

F Major

BOOK ONE

THIS FUGUE is written in a TRIPLE METER — three beats in each measure. Since in music the first note of every measure is accented, we count a triple meter like this: **1**, 2, 3, **1**, 2, 3, **1**, 2, 3, and so on.* The bold numeral **1** indicates the accented (first) beat. DOUBLE METER has two beats in each measure and is counted as follows: **1**, 2, **1**, 2, **1**, 2, and so on.

On rare occasions during pieces written in triple meter, composers will switch for a few measures to double meter and then switch back to triple meter. The switch to double meter is known as a HEMIOLA. It is accomplished as follows: instead of accenting every third beat, the composer accents every second beat. For example, two measures, which would normally consist of two groups of three, now consist of three groups of two:

The Hemiola

	First Measure	Second Measure
Normal	1 2 3	1 2 3
Hemiola	1 2 3	1 2 3

*Actually, the fugue begins on the third beat of the measure, so that if we start counting with the very first note of the piece we should count: 3, **1**, 2, 3, **1**, 2, 3, etc.

LISTENER'S GUIDE
to the F Major Fugue
WELL-TEMPERED CLAVIER
Book One

PRELUDE

This fast and lively prelude almost made my Top Ten Preludes.

VOICES

3

MAJOR FEATURES

Stretto.
Counterexpositions.

SPECIAL DEVICES

Counterexpositions, entries 4–6, 8–10, 11–13. The second two counterexpositions are in stretto.
Stretto. This is a fugue that uses stretto.
Hemiola. There is a hemiola for the entire coda. See the essay for an explanation of hemiola.

FORM

First entry in the alto; second entry in the soprano; codetta; third entry in the bass; first episode, short; first counterexposition: fourth entry in the soprano; fifth entry in the alto; sixth entry in the bass, seventh entry in the alto in stretto; second episode; second counterexposition, a counterexposition in stretto: eighth entry in the soprano in minor, ninth entry in the alto in stretto in minor, tenth entry in the bass in stretto in minor; two measures; third counterexposition, a counterexposition in stretto: eleventh entry in the bass in minor, twelfth entry in the alto in stretto in minor, thirteenth entry in the soprano in stretto in minor; third episode; fourteenth and last entry in the soprano in major; coda.

LISTENING HINT

The stretto entries are far enough apart so that it is easy to follow each voice as it enters, but not so far apart as to lose the tension of voices overlapping in stretto.

In this fugue we can keep counting along by threes until the coda. That's where Bach switches, for the remainder of the piece, to double meter by means of a hemiola. If we listen to either the bass or the soprano during the coda, we'll be able to follow along with the fugue, now moving in a double meter: 1, 2, 1, 2, 1, 2.

An intriguing question is why Bach chose to use a hemiola at all. After all, the hemiola has nothing to do with the motive. The hemiola also isn't essential to the fugue's overall structure, since Bach could certainly have ended the fugue without using it in the coda.

The arrangement of entries is very interesting in this fugue, with three counterexpositions, including two in stretto. A COUNTEREXPOSITION IN STRETTO is just a counterexposition in which the entries enter in stretto. The Listener's Guide tells us that the order of entry in all the counterexpositions is either highest to lowest — soprano, alto, bass — or lowest to highest — bass, alto, soprano. Bach used these readily recognizable orders of entry to make sure that the counterexpositions are easy to hear.

Point, Counterexposition

The EXPOSITION is the first section of a fugue. In the exposition, each voice in the fugue has the subject once.

A COUNTEREXPOSITION is a collection of entries of the subject, one in each voice, that occurs sometime in the fugue after the exposition.

A counterexposition and the exposition, however, use a *different* order of entry of the voices. For example, in the exposition of F Major Book One, a three-voice fugue, the voices enter alto, soprano, bass. In entries 8–10, a counterexposition, the voices enter soprano, alto, bass.

A REEXPOSITION is a collection of entries of the subject, one in every voice, that occurs sometime in a fugue after the exposition. In a reexposition the voices enter in the *same* order as in the exposition.

Because counterexpositions are difficult for the audience to hear, I expected to find Bach using them only on rare occasions. I thought the only fugues with counterexpositions were F Major Book One and a couple of fugues with a lot of stretto, such as C Major Book One, that sneaked a counterexposition into all those entries running in stretto.

I stand by my first point, that counterexpositions are difficult to hear. In the middle of a fugue with entries and episodes and countermaterial coming in all over the place, in three or more voices, it is tough to find a sufficient number of entries, one in every voice, to constitute a counterexposition.

On the second point I was dead wrong. Not only are counterexpositions not rare, they actually are quite common: 21 fugues in the *Well-Tempered*, 11 in Book One and 10 in Book Two, have counterexpositions.

FUGUES IN THE *WELL-TEMPERED* WITH COUNTEREXPOSITIONS

BOOK ONE	BOOK TWO
C Major	c minor
c-sharp minor	C-sharp Major
D Major	c-sharp minor
d-sharp minor	D Major
e minor	E-flat Major
F Major	d-sharp minor
F-sharp Major	E Major
A-flat Major	F-sharp Major
A Major	f-sharp minor
a minor	b-flat minor
B Major	

Some fugues have two, three, four, even five counterexpositions. Two fugues — a minor Book One and b-flat minor Book Two — with five each, are the counterexposition champions in the *Well-Tempered*.

I was surprised not only by the number of fugues with counterexpositions, but also by the number of ways in which Bach used them. In the *Well-Tempered* we find counterexpositions in stretto, those in which the voices run the melodic inversion of the subject, those in which some voices run the subject in melodic inversion and some voices run the original version of the subject, and counterexpositions in which the entries run in DIMINU-TION (all the notes in the subject are cut to half their original length).

REEXPOSITIONS are much easier to hear than counterexpositions, and their use is also much easier to understand.

Consider C-sharp Major Book One, which is divided almost equally into two sections. In the first half, Bach strictly alternates between entries of the subject and short episodes. In the second half, Bach begins with a huge triple episode consuming almost one fourth of the fugue. Following the triple episode, the subject returns in grand and dramatic fashion with a reexposition — actually an exact copy of the exposition, countersubjects and all. C-sharp Major Book One ends not long after the reexposition. Similarly, F-sharp Major Book One ends with a reexposition of the second subject. Bach finishes b-flat minor Book One with a reexposition in stretto of all five voices in the same highest to lowest — soprano I to bass — order of entries used in the exposition.

This use of reexpositions at the end of a fugue to reprise the exposition is known as DA CAPO, from the Italian for "from the head," or beginning, of the piece. In Bach's time, so-called da capo arias were common. A typical da capo aria begins with a fast-moving first section that is followed by a slower-moving second section. The aria concludes with an exact repeat, starting right at the beginning of the piece, of some or all of the music from the first section.

Six fugues in the *Well-Tempered* have reexpositions. Three use da capo style.

FUGUES IN THE *WELL-TEMPERED* WITH REEXPOSITIONS

DA CAPO STYLE	*NOT DA CAPO STYLE*
C-sharp Major Book One	d minor Book One
F-sharp Major Book One (second subject)	e minor Book One
b-flat minor Book One	c minor Book Two

Excluding e minor Book One (because it is a two-voice fugue so its options are severely limited), only two fugues in the *Well-Tempered,* d minor Book One and c minor Book Two, use reexpositions in a manner other than da capo style — that is, in the same common style in which Bach used counterexpositions.

Bach used over 50 counterexpositions — with a different order of entry of voices than the exposition — in the *Well-Tempered* in a mundane way, but only two reexpositions — with the same order of entries as in the exposition — in that same mundane style. Clearly, Bach wanted to reserve the order of entries of voices in the exposition for use in special — da capo — occasions.

f minor
BOOK ONE

KNOWING THAT bigger isn't always better and that two subjects can make a fugue far too long and complicated, Bach usually made his double fugues his most modest and reserved.

There are two basic ways to write a double fugue. One is for the two subjects to be exposed and developed separately and then combine in some fashion later in the fugue. The next fugue in the *Well-Tempered,* F-sharp Major Book One, is an excellent example of this kind of double fugue.

In the other type, exemplified by this fugue, f minor Book One, the two subjects are exposed together and always run together. The second subject, which always accompanies the first subject, seems at first like a countersubject but then becomes so prominent that we must call it a second subject. In this fugue the fast-moving second subject doesn't sound like a countersubject for long; very quickly it becomes even more prominent and even easier to hear than the first subject. As this fugue gets moving, it is much easier to hear and follow the second subject than the first. The second subject, which uses fast notes and rests, accompanies eight of the ten entries of the slow, very chromatic first subject.

The two subjects are compared in the chart on page 103.

LISTENER'S GUIDE
to the f minor Fugue
WELL-TEMPERED CLAVIER
Book One

PRELUDE

A great minor, singing quality.

VOICES

4

MAJOR FEATURE

This is a double fugue, the type in which the two subjects are exposed together and the second subject almost always accompanies the first subject. Since the second subject runs against all the entries of the first subject except the first and eighth, I don't indicate in the *Form* section which entry of the second subject is running.

SPECIAL DEVICES

Double fugue.

FORM

First entry of the first subject in the tenor; second entry of the first subject in the alto, second subject in the tenor; third entry of the first subject in the bass, second subject in the alto; codetta; fourth entry of the first subject in the soprano, second subject in the bass; first episode; fifth entry of the first subject in the tenor, second subject in the soprano; second episode; sixth entry of the first subject in the bass, second subject in the tenor; third episode; seventh entry of the first subject in the alto in major, second subject in the soprano; fourth episode; eighth entry of the first subject in the tenor in major; fifth episode; ninth entry of the first subject in the soprano in minor, second subject in the alto; sixth episode; tenth and last entry of the first subject in the bass, second subject in the soprano; coda.

LISTENING HINTS

1. The second subject is probably easier to follow and hear than the first.

2. The second subject doesn't run against the first or eighth entry.

3. This fugue is made easier to follow because in the middle section of the fugue the episodes and entries strictly alternate, with an episode between every two entries and an entry between every two episodes.

With its two subjects, this fugue gets fairly complicated. To compensate somewhat for that complexity, the fugue's overall structure is fairly simple in some key ways.

First, the entries and episodes in the middle section STRICTLY ALTERNATE. Between every two entries in the middle section there is an episode, and between every two episodes there is an entry. Strict alternation makes it easy to follow the middle section as it moves from entry to episode.

Second, Bach uses the same sequences in the first, second, and sixth episodes, to reduce the number of disparate, unfamiliar, and complex episodes that our ears have to follow.

The Two Subjects Compared

	Slow/Fast	*Chromatic/Not Chromatic*
First subject	slow	very chromatic
Second subject	fast	slightly chromatic

Another fugue in the *Well-Tempered* — E-flat Major Book One — uses strict alternation in its middle section and the same sequence in three different episodes. While this fugue is slow, emotional, and deliberate, E-flat Major Book One is quick, happy, and lively, which tells us that it's possible for fugues of strongly contrasting sensibilities to have a number of critical structural similarities.

Double Fugues

A DOUBLE FUGUE has two subjects. A TRIPLE FUGUE has three. There are eight double and two triple fugues in the *Well-Tempered*:

DOUBLE AND TRIPLE FUGUES IN THE *WELL-TEMPERED*

BOOK ONE	BOOK TWO
c-sharp minor (triple fugue)	c-sharp minor
f minor	f-sharp minor (triple fugue)
F-sharp Major	g-sharp minor
f-sharp minor	a minor
A Major	B Major

Here is a classification of all the double fugues from the *Well-Tempered* in terms of those in which subjects are exposed separately, and those in which the second subject at first seems like a countersubject.

Case I. The two subjects are exposed separately and then combine later in the fugue in all sorts of ways

F-sharp Major Book One
A Major Book One

Case Ia. The two subjects are exposed separately, but when they do combine the two subjects run only against each other, as in Case II below

g-sharp minor Book Two
B Major Book Two

Case Ib. The two subjects are exposed separately, and then hardly combine at all

c-sharp minor Book Two

Case II. The second subject at first seems like a countersubject, but then becomes so promi-nent — it often takes over the fugue — that we must call it a second subject, not a countersubject

f minor Book One
f-sharp minor Book One
a minor Book Two

I haven't even tried to calculate the number of possibilities and variations on those pos-sibilities for triple fugues. Luckily, we can just deal with the only two triple fugues in the *Well-Tempered* as they occur. Both expose all three subjects separately and then have the subjects combine in all sorts of different ways, very much like Case I above for double fugues.

The two subjects in Bach's double fugues, or three subjects in his triple fugues, are quite different (except for c-sharp minor Book Two, in which the second subject is built directly from the first). Typically, if one subject uses slow notes, the other uses fast notes. If one subject moves by steps, the other moves by jumps. If one subject uses a lot of chro-matic notes, the other uses hardly any. A prime example is the c-sharp minor fugue Book One. For more information see the essay on that fugue.

F–sharp Major

BOOK ONE

WE HAVE here one of the best, if not the very best, fugues in the entire *Well-Tempered,* a fugue that makes not only my Top Ten, but also my Superstar Four. What makes this fugue so great are the first and second subjects, and the way the two subjects fit and run together.

A Double Fugue?

I think this is a double fugue, despite the fact that the phrase I call the second subject is only two beats long. The question arises: is a two-beat phrase too puny to be a subject?

Let's compare this fugue with C-sharp Major Book Two. C-sharp Major Book Two is a three-voice fugue, like this one. Like the second subject of this fugue, C-sharp Major Book Two's subject is also only two beats long. The third and final voice to enter in the exposition of C-sharp Major Book Two is the alto, just as in the exposition of the second subject of this fugue. Finally, the entry in the alto in the exposition of C-sharp Major Book Two is the MELODIC INVERSION of the subject, just as is the entry in the alto in the exposition of the second subject of this fugue. These are the only two subjects in the *Well-Tempered* that have entries in melodic inversion during their expositions.

The chart illustrates the similarities between the second subject of this fugue and the subject of C-sharp Major Book Two.

LISTENER'S GUIDE
to the F-sharp Major Fugue
WELL–TEMPERED CLAVIER
Book One

PRELUDE

One of the very best. The bass line is eminently singable.

This two-part prelude would make an excellent violin/cello, flute/cello, or oboe/cello duet.

VOICES

3

MAJOR FEATURES

Double fugue.
Excellent first and second subjects.
Great sequential canonic episodes.

SPECIAL DEVICES

This is a double fugue in which the two subjects are exposed separately and then combine.

The fourth episode is a double episode, the first half of which is sequential and canonic.

The second and fifth episodes are canonic.

NOTE

The outline for the structure of this fugue is given by the entries of the first subject, as if this were just any plain old single fugue. "First episode" means first episode with respect to the first subject.

Not all the entries of the second subject are included in the Form section. See the essay for more on the second subject.

FORM

First entry of the first subject in the soprano; second entry of the first subject in the alto; third entry of the first subject in the bass; first episode (includes exposition of the second subject): first entry of the second subject in the soprano, second entry of the second subject in the bass, third entry of the second subject in the alto in melodic inversion; fourth entry of the first subject in the soprano; short second episode; fifth entry of the first subject in the alto; third episode; sixth entry of the first subject in the bass in minor; fourth episode, a double episode, the first half of the episode has a canon between the soprano and the alto; seventh entry of the first subject in the alto in major; fifth episode, canon between the soprano and the alto very similar to the canon in the second episode; eighth and last entry of the first subject in the soprano; coda: a reexposition of the second subject, soprano, bass, alto.

	Second Subject of This Fugue	Subject of C-sharp Major Fugue Book Two
Length	two beats	two beats
Number of voices	three	three
Order of entries	soprano, bass, alto	bass, soprano, alto
Alto entry	melodic inversion of the subject	melodic inversion of the subject

The Second Subject as an Integral Part of the Fugue's Structure

But even if two beats isn't a priori too short for a subject, it is necessary to demonstrate that the two-beat phrase I am calling the second subject is integrated in an important way into the structure of the fugue to justify calling it a second subject.

Let's look at a diagram of the structure of this fugue.

The Structure of F-sharp Major Book One

Exposition of the First Subject	First Half of the First Episode	Second Half of the First Episode
	exposition of the second subject	material from the second subject in the bass
Fourth Entry of the First Subject	*Second Episode*	*Fifth Entry of the First Subject*
material from the second subject in the bass	material from the second subject in the bass	
Third Episode	*Sixth Entry of the First Subject*	*First Half of the Fourth Episode*
counterexposition of the second subject	material from the second subject in the soprano	material from the second subject in the bass
In between the First and Second Half of the Fourth Episode		*Second Half of the Fourth Episode*
material from the second subject in the alto		material from the second subject in the soprano

Seventh Entry of the First Subject	Fifth Episode	Eighth Entry of the First Subject
material from the second subject first in the bass then in the soprano	material from the second subject in the bass	

Coda
reexposition of the second subject

As we can see, the material from what I call the second subject is extremely well integrated into this fugue, including an exposition, a counterexposition, and a reexposition. I think we can safely conclude that this is definitely a double fugue.

The Superstar Four

Along with a World Series championship, the pinnacle of any baseball player's career is induction into the Baseball Hall of Fame in Cooperstown, New York. It is the height of personal achievement. Two hundred or so of the legendary greats of the game have had their plaques enshrined there since the Hall of Fame opened its doors in 1939. They will be joined by stars from the present and the future. And while we all know of players that aren't in the Hall but should be (like Phil Rizzuto), almost without exception all the players who have been admitted deserve to be there and have made giant contributions to the game of baseball.

However, even among the select club that is the membership in the Baseball Hall of Fame, there is another much smaller group of players who deserve, if not their own hall, at least maybe their own separate room. This collection of "Hall of Fame" Hall of Famers includes players who have defined stardom and greatness in their time and for the future, such as Ty Cobb, Honus Wagner, Cy Young, Joe DiMaggio, Mickey Mantle, Willie Mays, and, of course, the man who took baseball itself onto his shoulders and transformed it once again into the Great American Game after the 1919 Black Sox scandal, the Bambino, George Herman "Babe" Ruth.

Within my Top Ten Fugues there is also a select group of pieces that I think are far better than the other fugues in the *Well-Tempered*, even than the rest of the Top Ten, fugues that never fail to inspire me or to lift my spirits and make me happy. I call these the SUPERSTAR FOUR. F-sharp Major Book One is a member, along with c minor Book One, C Major Book Two, and E-flat Major Book Two.

f–sharp minor

BOOK ONE

WHAT IS such a short, fast, lively prelude doing with such a long, slow, ponderous fugue?

This fugue, despite the incompatibly upbeat prelude that precedes it, and despite having two subjects, two codettas, no coda, just one episode, and being unique among the fugues in the *Well-Tempered* with respect to order of entries and time signature, is really (and I mean this quite sincerely) a fairly normal-sounding fugue.

This is a double fugue, the type in which the two subjects are exposed together. Since the second subject is so radically different in character from the first, and since the second subject is used so prominently throughout, we can't call it a countersubject and must call it a second subject.

Compare the long-held notes of the first subject with the repeated note figures of the second subject, noticing how prominent the repeated note figure is throughout the fugue — more prominent, even, than the material from the first subject — and you'll see why this is definitely a double fugue.

The repeated note figure used in the second subject is also used in the second subject of the F-sharp Major fugue Book One, in the second subject of the c minor fugue of the c minor Passacaglia and Fugue for Organ (BWV 582), and in the third subject of the eleventh fugue from the *Art of the Fugue.*

LISTENER'S GUIDE
to the f-sharp minor Fugue
WELL–TEMPERED CLAVIER
Book One

PRELUDE

This sounds very much like a violin piece because of the sequential figures in the upper parts and the chords in the upper part that would make excellent DOUBLE STOPS (when a violinist plays on more than one string at a time). This prelude would make an excellent violin/cello duet.

VOICES

4

MAJOR FEATURE

A double fugue, the type in which the two subjects are exposed together.

SPECIAL DEVICES

Double fugue.
Entries 5 and 8 are the melodic inversion of the subject.

FORM

First entry of the first subject in the tenor; second entry of the first subject in the alto, second subject in the tenor; first codetta; third entry of the first subject in the bass, second subject in the alto; second codetta (long); fourth entry of the first subject in the soprano, second subject in the bass; two and a half measures; fifth entry of the first subject in the alto in inversion; one and a half measures; sixth entry of the first subject in the soprano, second subject in the alto; one measure; seventh entry of the first subject in the tenor, second subject in the soprano (notice the pair of sixteenths in the soprano at the beginning of the entry, the only pair of sixteenths in the fugue); eighth entry of the first subject in the bass in inversion; first and only episode, a small canon involving all four voices, the tenor and alto lead, the soprano and bass follow; ninth and last entry of the first subject in the soprano, second subject in the alto and tenor; no coda.

LISTENING HINT

The second codetta is long, longer than the subject of this fugue.

Some "Onlys"

This is the only fugue in the *Well-Tempered* written in $\frac{6}{4}$ time. Only one prelude in the *Well-Tempered* is in $\frac{6}{4}$, c-sharp minor prelude Book One.

This is the only fugue in the *Well-Tempered* in which the order of entries of voices in the exposition is tenor, alto, bass, soprano.

This is one of only five fugues in the *Well-Tempered* that has not one but two codettas. The second codetta is longer than the subject. Only three other fugues in the *Well-Tempered* have codettas that are longer than the subject.

There is only one episode in this fugue: the two measures between the eighth and ninth entries of the first subject. These two measures are a canon involving all four voices, the only time in the *Well-Tempered* in which *four* voices take part in a canon. Usually, only two voices will take part in the canon, with the other voices either resting or free from the canon. The four voices work in pairs, with the alto and tenor as the leaders and the soprano and bass as the followers. The canon uses material from the second subject.

Finally, this fugue has only one pair of sixteenth notes. Those occur in measure 29, the first measure of the seventh entry of the first subject. The sixteenths are in the soprano, which has the second subject. See the following box for more on the number 29.

14 + 41 = 141

Let us recall the code in which A = 1, B = 2, C = 3, and so on. In this code B-A-C-H = 14, J-S-B (Bach's cufflinks) = 29, and J-S-B-A-C-H = 41. (To get the correct values for JSB and J. S. BACH remember that in the German alphabet of Bach's time I and J were the same letter.)

Let us also recall that in old German musical notation B stood for B-flat and H for B-natural. So Bach could, and did (as we will see), spell out his name with musical tones: B-flat, A, C, B-natural.

Now we are going to indulge in some more unabashed numerology by examining things like the fourteenth fugue in both books of the *Well-Tempered*, the twenty-ninth and forty-first measures of certain fugues, and musical phrases that happen to have 14 or 41 notes in them or that happen to go B-A-C-H.

Most discussions about numerology, while interesting, are generally regarded as nonsense. Even though there might be something curious and interesting in the forty-first measure of a certain piece or in the fourteenth piece of a collection of pieces, there is the general belief that if one only looks hard enough, something just as interesting, or even more interesting, can be found in the fortieth measure of a certain piece or in the fifteenth piece in a collection of pieces. Furthermore, if 14 spells "Bach," then we could probably find an important phrase spelled out by 15, or 13, or 24, or 414.

Even in the face of these valid objections, I am going to present 12 examples (not 14 — there is only so much strain my credibility can take) of 14's, 29's, and 41's in Bach's music. I believe that all these examples (well, except maybe for one) were put there deliberately by J. S. Bach, and that we can learn a great deal by considering why and what they are doing there.

Furthermore, I think that most people find numerology somewhat interesting, even though not everyone will admit it; and if Bach actually did put these 14's and 41's in his music, especially since we can hear some of them quite clearly even without any prompting, we have yet another example of the immense care with which Bach planned his pieces and the minute level of detail in which he did so.

As to why Bach put all these 14's and 41's in his music, I don't really know. It may have just been a desire to put his signature indelibly on some pieces, as artists will often do when they paint themselves into their pictures or as Hitchcock did when he made a cameo appearance in each of his movies.

1. Let's start right where Bach did, with his first published piece, a partita (suite) for clavier in B-flat Major (BWV 825). The first notes of this partita for both the left-hand and right-hand parts are B-flats. Three B-flats for Bach!

2, 3. A slightly more substantial example — make that two examples — occurs in the first fugue, the C Major fugue Book One of the *Well-Tempered*. The subject has 14 notes (count 'em). Also, of the 24 entries (remember, C Major Book One is the great stretto fugue), 22 run all the way to completion, and a twenty-third runs almost all the way to completion. Only one entry doesn't run anywhere near to completion, and which one do you think it is? You guessed it — the fourteenth. As I explained in my essay about C Major Book One, the fact that the fourteenth entry does not run all the way to completion is not just of anecdotal interest, but is important to the structure of the fugue.

4. "O.K., Eric," you say, "I agree that the 14's and the B-flat's you have mentioned are in the music, and they probably didn't get there by accident. But who can really hear the one entry out of 24 that doesn't run all the way to completion? Who actually counts the notes of the subject of a fugue while they are listening to it? If the partita had been in A Major and not B-flat Major, who could have told the difference?"

"Listen to the E Major prelude Book One," I respond. If you do, you'll hear that the whole prelude is written in slow notes — the whole prelude, that is, except one measure. One measure in the prelude, one measure that stands out like a Yankee fan at Fenway Park, one measure that you cannot possibly miss, has all fast notes. That measure is measure 14.

5, 6. Two more 14's: the fourteenth fugues (in f-sharp minor) in Book One and Book Two. Both are multiple fugues. The fourteenth in Book One is a double fugue, and the fourteenth in Book Two is a triple fugue. There are only ten double or triple fugues in the *Well-Tempered*. Two of those ten are the fourteenth fugues of Book One and Book Two. Just a coincidence? I think not. The odds that fugues 14 in both books would be double or triple fugues are less than 4 percent.

7. Let's move on from 14 to 29. We have to go back for a minute to the fourteenth fugue in Book One. In that entire fugue there are only two sixteenth notes. Guess in which measure the two sixteenths occur? Measure 29. The two sixteenths come at the beginning of the second subject in the soprano, which runs against the seventh entry of the first subject in the bass. The second subject runs five other times, but only uses the sixteenths this once.

8. Now up to 41, specifically the forty-first measure of the first fugue in Book Two. That fugue, in C Major, is written in $\frac{2}{4}$ time, which means that every measure has two

quarter notes. The fastest notes in the fugues are sixteenths. At four sixteenths per quarter note, that makes a maximum of eight sixteenths per measure. You can think of every measure having a maximum of eight slots, or holes, to fill. From measure 23 of the C Major fugue Book Two through the second to last measure, measure 81, each hole is filled in every measure — except in measure 41, which has one hole, or one missing sixteenth note. With the missing sixteenth note, Bach has left his signature in the first fugue in Book Two, just as he did in the first fugue in Book One. See the essay about C Major Book Two for more on the missing sixteenth.

9. Let's move on to three-digit numbers and figure out why 14 + 41 = 141. Consider the fugue from the Toccata, Adagio, and Fugue in C Major (BWV 564). It is 141 measures long. I might seem to be reaching a bit here, but the C Major fugue has an "extra" measure between the fifth and sixth and the sixth and seventh entries of the subject.

One explanation for these measures is definitely to add some variety to the fugue. The subject of the C Major organ fugue, at nine measures, is one of Bach's longest. The subject is exposed without any music (codettas) in between the four entries. After the exposition Bach has a short episode and then entries 5, 6, and 7 with one measure in between entries 5 and 6, and one between entries 6 and 7. The extra entries break up, just a bit, the monopoly of the subject in the C Major fugue. But another explanation is that Bach realized how long the fugue was and decided to add the extra measures to make sure that it totaled 141 measures.

10. We now move from numbers to letters: specifically, the letters B-A-C-H.

Throughout his life Bach had a penchant for complete, comprehensive, and encyclopedic coverage of musical ideas in his work. Examples include two complete year-long cycles of cantatas, which Bach wrote in 1723–24 and 1724–25, the first book of the *Well-Tempered Clavier,* and complete sets of six cello suites, violin sonatas, and partitas, and French Suites, English Suites, and partitas for harpsichord. As Bach grew older, his desire for comprehensive treatment of material within a given work became even greater. In the last ten years of his life Bach wrote many comprehensive sets of pieces. These include Book Two of the *Well-Tempered Clavier* (1742), the *Goldberg Variations* (1742), the Canonic Variations on *Vom Himmel hoch* (1747), the *Musical Offering* (1747), and, finally, Bach's most famous comprehensive set of pieces, the *Art of the Fugue,* also written in 1747.

The *Art of the Fugue* is a collection of 14 fugues and 4 canons, all with subjects based on the same theme. It is often said that the *Art of the Fugue* was written by Bach to demonstrate all possible fugal techniques. This is nonsense. There are many, many techniques in the *Well-Tempered,* the organ fugues, and the vocal and instrumental fugues. On the other hand, there are techniques in the *Art of the Fugue* not found anywhere else in Bach — for example, an entire fugue that can be mirror inverted and still be a good fugue. In the *Art of the Fugue* Bach demonstrates the possibilities for taking a single theme and working it out using a huge number of fugal techniques.

The fourteenth fugue in the *Art of the Fugue* was left unfinished by Bach. The fugue is at least a triple fugue, Bach having stopped writing just after the exposition of the third subject. Why was the fugue left unfinished? It is incorrectly believed by many that Bach died before being able to finish it, but historical evidence tells us that the *Art of the Fugue* was written by 1747, three years before Bach's death in 1750. Just as for Schubert's great Eighth Symphony, which is also unfinished, we will probably never know why Bach didn't finish the fourteenth fugue in the *Art of the Fugue*. There is also the possibility that even 14 fugues did not complete Bach's plan for the *Art of the Fugue*. We will never know.

The third subject of the fourteenth fugue from the *Art of the Fugue,* after the exposition of which Bach abandoned work on the piece, makes prominent use of a very curious collection of four notes: B-flat, A, C, B-natural.

11. The first subject of the c-sharp minor fugue in the *Well-Tempered* Book One has only four notes. Though in a different key, the four-note first subject of the c-sharp minor fugue from Book One has the same shape, with one exception, as B-A-C-H. If I could ever meet Bach, I would ask him whether it is just a coincidence that the first subject of the c-sharp minor fugue from Book One is similar to B-A-C-H, or whether it is a deliberate perturbation on his part of B-A-C-H.

12. We began this list where Bach did, and we end as Bach did: with his last piece.

As legend has it, Bach, having gone blind in the last few years of his life, dictated his final piece to his son-in-law, Johann Christoph Altnikol, while lying on his deathbed. The piece is a chorale prelude on the chorale *Vor deinen Thron tret'*.

CHORALE is the name for a hymn sung in Lutheran church services. A CHORALE PRELUDE was a short piece based on the week's chorale and played by the organist before the congregation sang the chorale. There are many different styles in which a chorale prelude can be written, the only requirement being that it somehow use the chorale melody.

Not entirely surprisingly, Bach decided to make his last chorale prelude a fugue for four voices. Three take part in the fugue, while the fourth and highest voice has the chorale melody. Bach broke up the melody from the hymn *Vor deinen Thron tret'* into four parts. Each of the four parts of the melody is used as a fugue subject, with an exposition and some middle section, and then each section of the melody runs in the soprano while the fugue is going on in the lower voices.

So *Vor deinen Thron tret'* is a *quadruple* fugue, the only one Bach wrote. Additionally, in each of the four expositions, the voice to enter second has the melodic inversion of the subject. Also, at the end of the fugue Bach strettos and adds an extra voice, quite an achievement even for someone who could see what the piece looked like on the page.

Finally, at this point the number of notes in the first phrase of the soprano part in the chorale, and the total number of notes in the soprano part, should be familiar ones to us. That's right, 14 and 41.

For more on this fugue, see "What a Life III" at B-flat Major Book Two.

G Major

BOOK ONE

MY FIRST impressions of the *Well-Tempered Clavier* were based on a CBS recording by Anthony Newman of Book One, battered by years of circulation in the New York City Public Library system. (Sadly, that album, still my favorite recording of Book One, is out of print.) The album contained two records, but all I used to listen to was side one of the first record. That side contained the first six preludes and fugues, but I was especially interested in the first three — C Major, c minor, and C-sharp Major — which at the time I thought were the best preludes and fugues in the *Well-Tempered* by a mile. (All three are still in the Top Ten.) I didn't really care too much for any of the other preludes and fugues, and I was forever lamenting that in a work as long as the *Well-Tempered,* the best came at its very beginning.

Then two fugues, F-sharp Major and this one, G Major, caught my ear. They had a wistful, hopeful, stirring quality that I couldn't quite put my finger on.

Since the first time I borrowed Newman's recording from the New York Public Library for the Performing Arts at Lincoln Center (I can't remember now why I borrowed it; at the time I was into Bach's cantatas), I have listened to the *Well-Tempered* a few thousand times. The more and more closely I listened to most of the fugues from the *Well-Tempered,* the more I liked them, even the slow ones from side two of Newman's recording. But the more closely I listened to G Major Book One, the less I liked it. It had too many strange

LISTENER'S GUIDE
to the G Major Fugue
WELL–TEMPERED CLAVIER
Book One

PRELUDE
One of the fastest preludes in the *Well-Tempered.*

VOICES
3

MAJOR FEATURES
The subject.
Stretto.

SPECIAL DEVICES
Stretto. This is a fugue that uses stretto.

A sequence that is used in four episodes — first, second, third, and fifth.

A counterexposition in inversion — entries 4 to 6.

FORM
First entry in the soprano; second entry in the alto; codetta; third entry in the bass; first episode, uses the four-times-used sequence; fourth entry in the alto in inversion; fifth entry in the soprano in inversion; sixth entry in the bass in inversion; second episode, uses the four-times-used sequence; seventh entry in the soprano in minor; one measure; eighth entry in the alto in inversion; third episode, uses the four-times-used sequence; ninth entry in the soprano in minor, tenth entry in the bass in stretto in minor; fourth episode; eleventh entry in the alto; fifth episode, uses the four-times-used sequence; twelfth entry in the bass in inversion; sixth episode; thirteenth entry in the alto in inversion, fourteenth entry in the soprano in stretto; coda.

features: a counterexposition in inversion, lots of entries not running to completion, and an unusual amount of stretto, just to name a few.

If I don't listen too closely, it still has that same wonderful, wistful quality that it had the first time I listened to it. If I listen too closely, things are not so good.

g minor
BOOK ONE

———

DID YOUR grandfather constantly repeat to you the story of how, when he was a boy, he had to walk four miles in the snow to school? Did the same thing always incite him to tell the story — a heavy snowfall or your return from school? Do you, or does someone you know, not only smoke a lot, but always smoke at the same times, for example, with coffee in the morning?

If you can relate to either of the situations above, you have already had first-hand experience with motivicness *on top of* motivicness, which I call SECOND-ORDER MOTIVICNESS. Not only did your grandfather always tell the same story (motivicness), but the same thing always triggered the telling (second-order motivicness). Not only do some people smoke a lot of cigarettes (motivicness), but they smoke them on the same occasions (second-order motivicness). This fugue is one of the finest examples of second-order motivicness.

The Subject

The subject of this fugue, like so many subjects in the *Well-Tempered,* is in two parts. The first half of the subject consists of three eighth notes and two quarter notes. Then comes a rest. After the rest is the second half of the subject, two groups of three notes each. Each group of three notes consists of two sixteenth notes followed by one eighth note. The notes in the first group of three ascend by step. The second group of three descend by step.

LISTENER'S GUIDE
to the g minor Fugue
WELL-TEMPERED CLAVIER
Book One

PRELUDE

Excellent, ever so slightly reminiscent of the g minor movements in the *Goldberg Variations,* though this prelude is not nearly as chromatic or heavy as the movements in the *Goldbergs.* Member of my Top Ten Preludes.

VOICES

4

MAJOR FEATURES

Stretto.

Stretto always fits in the same place. See the essay for more on this.

An excellent move to the relative major and five entries (entries 5 through 9) in the relative major.

SPECIAL DEVICES

Ultraconsistent countersubject.

Stretto. This is a fugue that uses stretto. There is one stretto entry in the middle of the fugue (entry 9), and a stretto section at the end (entries 12 through 14).

A canon in inversion in the second half of the second episode.

FORM

First entry in the alto; second entry in the soprano, countersubject in the alto; codetta; third entry in the bass, countersubject in the soprano; fourth entry in the tenor, countersubject in the bass; first episode, great move to the relative major; fifth entry in the alto in major, countersubject in the tenor; sixth entry in the bass in major, countersubject in the tenor; seventh entry in the soprano in major, countersubject in the bass; half a measure; eighth entry in the bass in major, countersubject in the soprano, ninth entry in the alto in stretto in major; one measure, move back to minor; tenth entry in the bass in minor, countersubject in the alto (all entries are in minor from here to the end); eleventh entry in the soprano, countersubject in the bass; second episode, note the canon in inversion between the soprano and alto in the second half of this episode; stretto section: twelfth entry in the soprano, countersubject in the alto, thirteenth entry in the tenor in stretto, fourteenth entry in the bass in stretto; one measure; fifteenth entry in the alto, countersubject in the bass; sixteenth and last entry in the tenor; no coda.

The Countersubject

The countersubject of this fugue is in three parts. We will be most interested in the first two parts.

The first part is just a rest. The second part of the countersubject, like the second part of the subject, contains two groups of three notes, each group consisting of two sixteenth notes followed by an eighth note. However, unlike the second part of the subject, which first ascended by step and then descended by step, the second part of the countersubject first descends by step and then ascends by step. The third part of the countersubject is just five eighth notes moving by jumps. The second part of the subject and the second part of the countersubject are melodic inversions of each other.

"Counter" is part of the word *countersubject* to indicate that the countersubject is material that runs against the subject. The first part of the countersubject of this fugue is just a rest; so the countersubject really doesn't start running against the subject until the second part of the countersubject begins — the second half of the first quarter note in the subject.

The Stretto and Motivicnesses

This fugue strettos in two places. There is one pair of entries in stretto in the middle of the fugue, entries 8 and 9, and three entries in stretto, entries 12 through 14, toward the end of the fugue.

The second-order motivicness in this fugue is very simple: not only is the motive of the fugue, the subject, running against itself (motivicness), but every time that happens the voice entering with the entry of the subject in stretto enters in the same place in relation to the voice already running the subject (second-order motivicness). The audience can actually hear second-order motivicness, can actually hear that the stretto entries always enter in the same place.

Three guesses where the voice running the entry of the subject in stretto enters in relation to the voice already running the subject. That's right, the same place where the countersubject starts running against the subject.

The countersubject of this fugue is very, very consistent. It runs against every entry of the subject except the entries that run in stretto. When the stretto entries are present en masse at the end of the fugue, the countersubject is absent, and vice versa. Both the countersubject and the stretto entries begin running against the original entry of the subject in exactly the same place.

All the entries in stretto begin running against the voice already running the subject in the same place. All of the entries in stretto also begin running against the subject in the same place that the countersubject starts running against the subject. We know that the place where the countersubject and the entries in stretto start running against the voice already running the subject is during the first quarter note in the first half of the subject. But why there? What is so special about the first quarter note in the first half of the subject?

To appreciate the second-order and THIRD-ORDER MOTIVICNESS in this fugue, we had to focus on the rhythmic values of the notes in the subject and countersubject. To see what is so special about the spot where all the entries in this fugue start strettoing, we have to focus on the pitches of the notes in the subject.

Because this fugue is in g minor, we call g the TONIC NOTE of this piece. (When a piece is in c minor, we call c the tonic note of the piece. When a piece is in B Major then we call B the tonic note, and so on.) In fact, all the notes of a piece in a certain key are given names. (For example, the note five steps higher than the tonic note is known as the DOMINANT NOTE. The dominant note of the g minor fugue is d.) To understand why Bach strettos where he does in this fugue, we only have to know about the tonic note, and a note called the leading tone.

The LEADING TONE of a key is just one half step lower than the tonic note of the key. As its name implies, the job of the leading tone is to lead to the tonic. Basically, a leading tone in a musical piece is just dying to move to its tonic. The leading tone of g minor is F-sharp. For pieces in g minor, F-sharps can't wait to move to G's. The first quarter note of the subject of this fugue, the note in the middle of which Bach always starts strettoing, is an F-sharp, the leading tone of g minor. (Now we can finally see why Bach started strettoing during the first quarter note in the subject.)

As we know, when a fugue strettos, two or more voices run the subject at the same time. However, in the audience we are only really able to follow one voice at a time. So the true interest and power of stretto is that we want to hear both voices running the subject at the same time, and this is what we strain to hear — unsuccessfully — when we listen to stretto entries. Because we fail in our attempt to hear both voices running the subject at the same time, we want to hear the fugue again. We hope that the next time we will be able to follow all the voices simultaneously running the subject. Of course, the next time we can't follow all of the voices either, so we try again. And again. And again.

Let's suppose for a minute that Bach had started strettoing *after* the first quarter note. That would give Bach two possibilities: (1) start strettoing on the second quarter note; (2) start strettoing during the second half of the subject. Here is why both of these possibilities are terrible.

From the beginning of the subject until the start of the first quarter note, our attention is riveted on the subject. We sit on the edge of our chairs waiting for the first quarter note, on the leading tone, to move to the second quarter note on the tonic. However, once the subject moves to the second quarter note on the tonic, it gets a lot less interesting, and we don't follow the subject with nearly the zest with which we followed the subject before the second quarter note. If the stretto started after the first quarter note, when the second voice entered in stretto with the subject, we would follow the second voice and not care too much about the first voice, since the first voice just has the uninteresting part of the subject. But then the stretto would lose all its power, which comes when we try, unsuccessfully, to follow more than one voice at a time.

Since Bach started strettoing *on* the first quarter note, the stretto retains all of its power. When the second voice enters in stretto with the subject, we are still intently following the first voice waiting for the leading tone in that voice to move to the tonic. Therefore, Bach must start strettoing *on or before* the first quarter note. Of course, Bach could have strettoed before the first quarter note. He didn't because the most exciting place to stretto is on the leading tone.

Wake Up, Mozart

Like most of us — though it would be difficult to tell from the incredible amount of music he wrote in only thirty-five years — Mozart was lazy, and as a child he didn't like to get out of bed in the morning. His mother woke him up by playing on the piano the first seven notes of a major scale, stopping on the leading tone. Since Mozart could not stand the sound of a leading tone without the note it was leading to, he was forced to get out of bed, run to the piano, and play the note to which the leading tone was leading. And once Mozart did that, he was up!

A–flat Major

BOOK ONE

IF EVERYONE spoke with the same accent as everyone else, what would we lose? On the one hand, not very much. After all, people would still be saying the same things they were before: the content would not have changed. We might even gain something, since now it would be easier for everyone to understand everyone else.

On the other hand, we would lose a lot. We would lose the varying flavor of different accents, and the sense of the different cultures that produced those accents. Once accents had been absent for a long time, it would be hard even to understand the roles different accents played and their importance in earlier cultures and literature.

In music we don't have to imagine what would happen if accents disappeared. In one important way, they already have. Since the nineteenth century, even a little before, an equally tempered scale or tuning system has been used exclusively. This tuning system is most familiar to us as the tuning system of the modern piano.

In "What Is the *Well-Tempered Clavier?*" we said that an EQUALLY TEMPERED tuning system is one in which the relationships between all the notes in a key are the same for every key. For example, in an equally tempered tuning system the relationship between the first note and the fifth note of the C major scale or the g minor scale is the same as the relationship between the first note and the fifth note of any key. Similarly, the relationship between the first note and the second note of a scale is the same as the relationship between the first note and the second note of any other scale, and so on for the relationship between any pair of notes.

LISTENER'S GUIDE
to the A-flat Major Fugue
WELL–TEMPERED CLAVIER
Book One

PRELUDE

Almost makes my Top Ten Preludes. I especially like the way it strettos.

VOICES

4

MAJOR FEATURE

A subject that jumps up, then down, then up again, then down again.

SPECIAL DEVICE

Sequential episodes.

FORM

First entry in the tenor; second entry in the bass; long codetta; third entry in the soprano; fourth entry in the alto; first episode; fifth entry in the tenor; second episode, sequential; sixth entry in the alto in minor; third episode; seventh entry in the tenor in minor; fourth episode fake entry in the alto; eighth entry in the alto; one measure; ninth entry in the alto; tenth entry in the soprano; fifth episode; eleventh entry in the bass; twelfth entry in the tenor; thirteenth entry in the alto; fourteenth entry in the soprano; sixth episode; fifteenth and last entry in the soprano; coda.

LISTENING HINT

The subject may be hard to follow.

All equal-tempered tuning systems are well-tempered, but not all well-tempered tuning systems are equally tempered. A well-tempered tuning system is one in which all keys can be used, as is possible in an equally tempered tuning system. However, there are tuning systems in which all keys can be used — i.e., well-tempered tuning systems — that are not equally tempered.

An equally tempered tuning system differs from well-tempered tuning systems commonly in use before the nineteenth century, in which the relationships between pairs of notes differed from key to key. For example, in a well-tempered tuning system that isn't equally tempered the relationship between the first and second notes of a key differed from key to key. Thus, each key had its own individual character and feeling. These differences among keys led to some subtle but very interesting features in music written for well-tempered but not equally tempered instruments. These nuances are lost when such music is played on an equally tempered instrument. When a piece played on a well- but not equally tempered instrument changes key, it really does change to a subtly but fundamentally different key. On an equally tempered instrument changing key just means moving up or down to another copy of the original key.

In modern times it may be hard to fathom that there could possibly be differences among keys, since equal tempering has been in use for so long. Yet some of the differences among keys were so well known and codified that composers deliberately wrote music in a certain style to fit the "reputation" of the key (see essay at f minor Book Two). These differences in compositional style are retained even when the piece is subsequently played on an equally tempered instrument, and can provide us today with interesting evidence about the differences between keys in well- but not equally tempered tuning systems.

A-flat Major is a wimpy-sounding key, as demonstrated by this fugue, A-flat Major Book One, and the A-flat Major fugue Book Two. Bach wrote an earlier version of A-flat Major Book Two in F Major. The F Major version, owing to differences arising from the keys in a well- but not equally tempered tuning system, sounds much stronger.

But we can't blame the wimpy sound of the A-flat Major fugue solely on the features and reputation of A-flat Major in a well-tempered tuning system. There are at least four other factors explaining the unfocused sound of this fugue:

The subject jumps. It jumps up, down, up, down, then up, then down, then all around. All it does is jump, with nary a single move by step. Despite all its jumping it never seems to get anywhere, contributing strongly to the feeling that the entire fugue is wandering.

This fugue has a sequence, used three different times, that also wanders. Listen to either the soprano in the second episode, the bass in the third episode, or the alto in the fourth episode. (See the Listener's Guide. The bass in the third episode is probably the easiest to hear.) The sequence goes up, then down, then up, then up, then down, then up. Since this sequence is used in three different episodes, it is no coincidence that this fugue sounds as if it is wandering.

A third reason that this fugue sounds as if it never quite gets moving is because in one important way it never does. If you listen closely you can notice that for the first 20 out of 35 measures (58 percent of the fugue) no single voice has the running sixteenth notes for more than a few measures before handing them off to another voice. So the fugue seems constantly to start and stop as one voice finishes with the running sixteenth notes and another voice takes its sweet time starting up with the sixteenth notes.

Finally, the first two thirds of this fugue strictly alternate between episodes and entries but never focus on a long double or triple episode or on two or more entries coming in a row.

The best way to listen to this fugue is to try to hear it in two parts: the first two thirds and then the last third.

The last 40 percent of this fugue is much more focused. The wandering sequence occurs only in the first 22 measures (episodes 2, 3, and 4) and not in the last 13 measures. In the last 13 measures most of the running sixteenths are in the lower two parts. In the first 22 measures the running sixteenths were handed off between the upper parts and the lower parts. Most important, in terms of alternation of episodes and entries, the last 13 measures are much more focused. While the first 22 measures wander indecisively, alternating strictly between episodes and entries, the last 13 measures move to a climax, first with a pair of entries (entries 9 and 10) and then with a counterexposition with a lowest to highest — bass to soprano — order of entries (entries 11 to 14).

The last 13 measures make a strong and decisive move to the counterexposition. But how does that help us with the wandering first 22 measures?

Well, let's think about what happens when you buy an album because there is one song in the album you like. At first, you listen only to the one song. After a while, you start listening to the song that comes before the song you like. Soon you start to like that one too. Then you start to listen to the song that comes after the song you bought the album for. You start to think that song isn't so bad either. Eventually, you may very well come to like all the songs in the album.

In the same way, we should consider the first 22 wandering measures as heading, very slowly and circuitously, toward the last 13 measures. Eventually, as we come to like the last 13 measures more and more, we start even to appreciate the first 22.

Codettas

As I said in "What Is a Fugue?" a codetta is any music that comes in between entries during the exposition. The codetta in a fugue comes between the second and third entries of the subject. Additionally, there are a few fugues in the *Well-Tempered* that have more than one codetta or that have a codetta between the third and fourth entries (or even between the fourth and fifth entries).

CODETTAS IN THE *WELL-TEMPERED*

	BOOK ONE	BOOK TWO
Fugues with codettas	17	19
Fugues without codettas	7	5
Fugues with one codetta	14	17
Fugues with two codettas	3	2
Codettas between entries 2 and 3	15	19
Codettas between entries 3 and 4	4	2
Codettas between entries 4 and 5	1	0

The question of the difference between a codetta and an episode can occasionally be tricky. Indeed, four fugues in the *Well-Tempered* — f-sharp minor Book One, A-flat Major Book One, b-flat minor Book One, and F Major Book Two — have codettas that are longer than the subjects of the fugues. In all four of these fugues the lengthy codetta does sound like an episode, rather than like the other, shorter codettas in the *Well-Tempered*. So, while in general codettas and episodes are distinct, the rare codetta that is longer than its subject is just an episode that happens to come during the exposition. But to avoid confusion I will still call the episodes that come during the exposition codettas.

g–sharp minor

BOOK ONE

BACH USES the last five notes of the subject 24 times in this fugue.

Let's compare the overall structure of this fugue with Bach's use of the five-note figure:

Structure of g-sharp minor Book One and the Five-Note Figure

Structural Unit	Number of Times Bach Uses the Five-Note Figure
first entry	1
second entry	1
third entry	1
fourth entry	1
first episode	2
fifth entry	1
second episode	2
sixth entry	1
seventh entry	1
eighth entry	1
third episode	0
ninth entry	1
tenth entry	1
first half of the fourth episode	0
second half of the fourth episode	2
eleventh entry	1
fifth episode	5
twelfth entry	1
coda	1
TOTAL	24

LISTENER'S GUIDE
to the g-sharp minor Fugue
WELL–TEMPERED CLAVIER
Book One

PRELUDE

Excellent, a member of my Top Ten Preludes. Notice that the whole piece is spun out of the first six notes in the soprano.

VOICES

4

MAJOR FEATURE

The last five notes of the subject.

SPECIAL DEVICES

Sequential episodes.
Sequential canonic episodes.

FORM

First entry in the tenor; second entry in the alto; third entry in the soprano; fourth entry in the bass; first episode; fifth entry in the tenor; second episode; sixth entry in the bass; seventh entry in the tenor; eighth entry in the alto; third episode; ninth entry in the soprano; tenth entry in the bass; fourth episode, a double episode; eleventh entry in the tenor; fifth episode; twelfth entry in the soprano; coda.

LISTENING HINT

The five uses of the five-note figure in the fifth episode really stand out.

Though he uses the five-note figure in every section except in the third episode and the first half of the fourth episode, he never uses it gratuitously or as a purely ornamental figure. Therefore, while it is used throughout the fugue, it still seems that Bach has employed the five-note figure sparingly.

The use of the five-note figure *five* times in the fifth episode is particularly noticeable, since the five-note figure isn't used more than twice in any other section of this fugue.

The absence of the five-note figure in the third episode and the first half of the double fourth episode makes its return in the second half of the fourth episode especially dramatic.

A Major

BOOK ONE

THIS DOUBLE fugue is the type in which the two subjects are exposed separately and combine later in the fugue. Of all such double fugues in the *Well-Tempered*, this one is the easiest in which to follow the separate expositions of the two subjects, and the section of the fugue in which the subjects combine. There are two reasons.

First: the two subjects are extremely distinctive. The first subject is composed of fairly slow-moving eighth notes and moves predominantly by jumps. The second subject is made up totally of faster sixteenth notes and almost always moves by step.

Also, the head of each subject stands out. The first subject begins with an eighth note followed by a rest for three eighth notes, an interesting way to begin a fugue — with silence. The sixteenth notes at the beginning of the second subject cascade downward and herald the start of the exposition of the second subject. I love these sixteenth notes. The first time I heard this fugue I thought it might be interesting, the intricate feeling of all three voices running against each other in eighth notes at the beginning of the fugue, and also occasional hints of small canons. Then the second subject entered with downward-moving sixteenth notes, rushing down like a wave. As the second subject began ascending, the wave headed upward, then downward again, and upward. . . .

Second: this fugue, in three sections, has a manageable overall structure. The first section, like the first subject, is dominated by eighth notes, with only three small groups of sixteenth notes in the 21 measures, which contain seven entries of the first subject.

LISTENER'S GUIDE
to the A Major Fugue
WELL–TEMPERED CLAVIER
Book One

PRELUDE
Almost makes my Top Ten Preludes. I especially like its canonic beginning.

VOICES
3

MAJOR FEATURE AND SPECIAL DEVICE
Double fugue.

The fugue has three sections. The first section contains the exposition of the first subject, four other entries of the first subject, and the first episode. In the second section the second subject is exposed and the first and second subjects combine. In the first half of the third section Bach uses material only from the first subject. In the second half of the third section Bach brings the fugue to a close using material from the second subject.

FORM
First section: first entry of the first subject in the soprano, second entry of the first subject in the alto; third entry of the first subject in the bass; one measure; fourth entry of the first subject in the bass; one measure; fifth entry of the first subject in the soprano; two measures; sixth entry of the first subject in the bass in minor; one measure; seventh entry of the first subject in the bass in minor; first episode.

Second section: eighth entry of the first subject in the soprano in minor, ninth entry of the first subject in the alto in stretto in minor, first entry of the second subject in the alto, tenth entry of the first subject in the bass in major; eleventh entry of the first subject in the alto, twelfth entry of the first subject in the bass in stretto; second entry of the second subject in the bass, thirteenth entry of the first subject in the alto in stretto; third entry of the second subject in the soprano; fourth entry of the second subject in the bass; fourteenth entry of the first subject in the tenor; fifteenth entry of the first subject in the bass; second episode (long); sixteenth entry of the first subject in the bass; one measure.

Third section: first half of the third section: seventeenth entry of the first subject in the alto; eighteenth entry of the first subject in the bass; third episode.

Second half of the third section: fifth entry of the second subject in the soprano; sixth entry of the second subject in the bass; coda.

LISTENING HINT
The first subject contains only slow notes moving mostly by jumps. The second subject contains only fast notes moving mainly by steps. It should be very easy to tell them apart.

You can't miss hearing the second section and the sixteenth-note-laden second subject. The second section makes extensive use of sixteenth notes, both those within four entries of the second subject, and other sixteenth notes not contained in any entry of the subject. Unlike the first section, the second section uses a variety of rhythms. Besides the four entries of the second subject, the second section contains nine entries of the first subject. The second subject is exposed and the two subjects combine in the second section of this fugue.

The third section of this fugue has two parts: the first half of the third section, containing no sixteenth notes, brings us back to the feeling and texture of the first section. In the second half of the third section the sixteenth notes and the second subject return to bring the fugue to a close.

a minor

BOOK ONE

THIS FUGUE is sprawling in terms of the amount of material in the subject, the number of entries of the subject, and its length.

The subject moves by steps and jumps. It uses fast notes, slower notes, and even uses a rest. The subject moves up, then down, then up again, then down again. It begins by using one pattern. After the rest, the subject uses another pattern. It's hard to believe that the subject of this fugue is only three measures long.

This fugue has *37* entries of the subject, including 17 entries of its melodic inversion of the subject. Only C-sharp Major Book Two, with 44 entries, has more. No other fugue in the *Well-Tempered* has more than 30 entries of the subject.

At 87 measures this fugue is tied with d-sharp minor Book One for eighth longest in the *Well-Tempered.* At over four and a half minutes of performance time, this fugue is one of the three or four longest fugues in the *Well-Tempered* to perform.

Fortunately, in two ways — where the stretto entries enter in relation to the voice already running the subject, and the organization of the entries — this fugue is not so sprawling that the audience cannot follow it.

All the stretto entries are on the sixth note of the voice already running the subject. See the Listener's Guide and listen closely to the fugue beginning with the ninth entry. If you count carefully, you should be able to hear the tenth entry of the subject entering on the sixth note of the ninth entry, the twelfth entry entering on the sixth

LISTENER'S GUIDE
to the a minor Fugue
WELL–TEMPERED CLAVIER
Book One

PRELUDE

This prelude and fugue are an odd couple: the prelude is one of the shortest and simplest, while the fugue is one of the longest and most complex in the *Well-Tempered*.

VOICES

4

MAJOR FEATURES

Very long fugue.

This fugue has 37 entries of the subject. Only C-sharp Major Book Two has more.

Stretto.

SPECIAL DEVICES

Stretto. This is a fugue that uses stretto.

Counterexpositions.

FORM

First entry in the alto; second entry in the soprano; codetta; third entry in the bass; fourth entry in the tenor; half a measure; fifth entry in the soprano in inversion; half a measure; sixth entry in the tenor in inversion; seventh entry in the bass in inversion; half a measure; eighth entry in the alto in inversion; half a measure; ninth entry in the soprano not inverted, tenth entry in the tenor in stretto; eleventh entry in the alto, twelfth entry in the bass in stretto; one and a half measures; thirteenth entry in the tenor, fourteenth entry in the alto in stretto; three measures; fifteenth entry in the soprano, sixteenth entry in the bass in stretto; two measures; seven-

teenth entry in the alto in inversion, eighteenth entry in the tenor in stretto in inversion; one measure; nineteenth entry in the bass in inversion, twentieth entry in the soprano in stretto in inversion; one measure; twenty-first entry in the soprano in inversion, twenty-second entry in the alto in stretto in inversion; three and a half measures; twenty-third entry in the bass not inverted, twenty-fourth entry in the tenor in stretto; twenty-fifth entry in the soprano in inversion, twenty-sixth entry in the alto in stretto in inversion; two and a half measures; twenty-seventh entry in the bass in inversion, twenty-eighth entry in the soprano in stretto in inversion; twenty-ninth entry in the tenor in inversion, thirtieth entry in the alto in stretto, thirty-first entry in the soprano in stretto; pause; thirty-second entry in the alto, thirty-third entry in the soprano in stretto; pause; thirty-fourth entry in the tenor in inversion, thirty-fifth entry in the alto in stretto in inversion, thirty-sixth entry in the soprano in stretto not inverted, thirty-seventh and last entry in the alto in stretto, coda.

LISTENING HINTS

1. This fugue has pauses after the thirty-first and the thirty-third entries.

2. The melodic inversion of the subject of this fugue is easy to hear.

3. Until the end of the fugue the stretto entries come in pairs.

4. It should be easy to differentiate between the entries of the subject and the material between the subjects.

note of the eleventh entry, and so on. Also, there are never more than two entries of the subject running in stretto at the same time until the very end of the fugue, when the last four entries run in stretto.

The first 28 entries of the subject, organized in groups of four, include four counterexpositions. Each counterexposition in this four-voice fugue, of course, contains four entries of the subject further broken down into two pairs of entries. Pairs of entries dominate until the end of the fugue.

As usual, Bach compensates for one part of the piece being long and complicated by making other components especially simple and easy to follow.

Did Bach ever try a sprawling fugue like this again, or did he consider this kind of piece an experiment not worth repeating? Yes, he did try a fugue like this again: C-sharp Major Book Two, which is similar to this fugue in an interesting way. As I mentioned, C-sharp Major Book Two, with 44 entries of the subject, is the only fugue in the *Well-Tempered* with more entries than this one. C-sharp Major Book Two has entries of the subject in inversion, in stretto, and in DIMINUTION (all the rhythmic values of notes in the subject are made shorter). C-sharp Major Book Two even has some entries in both inversion and diminution.

Thanksgiving at the WELL-TEMPERED's

In most of the Listener's Guide we have discussed the structure of individual fugues. But disk jockeys talk not only about individual songs but also about connections between and among songs. Here we're going to examine the family relationships among the fugues in the *Well-Tempered*.

When we look through the *Well-Tempered* for connections, we notice something strange: except for c minor Book One and C Major Book Two, there aren't any other obvious connections among pieces in the *Well-Tempered*. The subjects of c minor Book One and C Major Book Two start out the same way; both fugues have four sequential episodes, and the fourth episode in both fugues is a classic sequential canonic episode that starts out just like the first episode.

So at first blush, the fugues from the *Well-Tempered* seem almost completely unrelated. The *Well-Tempered Clavier* does not have the complex internal organization that some of Bach's other works do — for example, the *Goldberg Variations*. But closer scrutiny of the *Well-Tempered* reveals some subtle connections.

Unlike the music of most composers who came after Bach, the structure of Bach's pieces is often very difficult to understand, let alone discern what it is about the structure of a particular piece that helps make it so wonderful. Bach used such a wide variety of musical forms, including many that date from before his time and whose origin is no longer known, that it can be difficult to describe the form of some of Bach's pieces on even the most basic level.

Yet connections definitely exist among all of Bach's pieces. Listed here are groups of fugues from the *Well-Tempered* that are related to one another in various ways — families of fugues, you might say. The families are divided into two parts.

PART I

Here are fugues drawn from all over the *Well-Tempered* that are related by one or more family traits.

The First Family

> c minor Book One
> E-flat Major Book One
> C Major Book Two
> f minor Book Two

These four fugues form the most prominent family in the *Well-Tempered*. All are SIMPLE FUGUES having utterly clear distinctions between episodes and entries. All have sequential episodes; all but f minor Book Two have sequential canonic episodes. The beginnings of the subjects of c minor Book One and C Major Book Two are virtually the same: these two fugues are first cousins. For more on this family see f minor Book Two.

An Old Style

> E-flat Major Book Two
> E Major Book Two
> B Major Book Two

These three fugues are written in an old style (old even in the time of Bach). All three have the same time signature — $\frac{2}{2}$ — the same order of entries — lowest to highest, bass to soprano — and a predominance of slower note values, all common features of fugues written before Bach.

Another Old Style

> c-sharp minor Book One
> b-flat minor Book One

These two fugues are the only five-voice fugues in the *Well-Tempered*. They are written in an old style different from that of E-flat Major Book Two, E Major Book Two, and B Major Book Two.

The Long, Slow, and Not My Favorite Club

> b minor Book One (president of the club)
> c-sharp minor Book One
> d-sharp minor Book One

The name of this family says it all.

A Progression

> b-flat minor Book One
> d-sharp minor Book One
> a minor Book One

These three fugues, in the order listed above, form what seems like an historical progression of slow fugues in minor with a lot of stretto. B-flat minor Book One is in the oldest style, written in $\frac{2}{2}$ with five voices in a highest to lowest order of entries, using half notes and quarter notes almost exclusively and an incredibly square subject. D-sharp minor Book One has a more daring subject, and employs throughout eighth notes, dotted eighth notes, and even some sixteenths. In the long, windy, wonderful, and intricate a minor Book One, all bets are off.

Two-by-Two

> g minor Book Two
> b-flat minor Book Two

These are the two fugues in the *Well-Tempered* that make significant use of stretto entries that overlap completely. Both fugues also have very long subjects with lots of rests.

Strict Alternation

> E-flat Major Book One
> f minor Book One

It is most surprising to see such a happy and lively fugue as E-flat Major Book One and such a slow and emotional fugue as f minor Book One having anything in common.

PART II

These families of fugues come pretty much in the order of the *Well-Tempered* itself.

They're Off

> C Major Book One
> c minor Book One
> C-sharp Major Book One

> c-sharp minor Book One
> D Major Book One
> d minor Book One

I love five of the first six fugues in the *Well-Tempered* (I really don't like the c-sharp minor). The first three fugues are in the Top Ten.

Double Trouble

> f minor Book One
> F-sharp Major Book One
> f-sharp minor Book One

All three, which come in a row, are double fugues.

A Feeling

> F-sharp Major Book One
> G Major Book One
> g minor Book One prelude
> A Major Book One

These three fugues and one prelude all have a certain wistful feeling.

Three Heads I

> B-flat Major Book One
> B Major Book One

The heads of the subjects of both these fugues make prominent use of a three-note figure.

Three Heads II

> c-sharp minor Book Two
> d minor Book Two

The heads of the subjects of these two fugues make prominent use of triplets.

Yawn

> a minor Book One
> b-flat minor Book One
> B Major Book One
> b minor Book One

These are four of the last five fugues from Book One of the *Well-Tempered Clavier*. (The wonderful, happy, and short B-flat Major Book One is the only one of the last five fugues in Book One that isn't listed above.) Book One, closing with all these long, slow fugues, sure ends with a whimper. The action doesn't really get going again until C Major Book Two.

B-flat Major

BOOK ONE

OPEN THE baseball records book to the name Berra, Lawrence Peter, and you'll find some pretty impressive statistics: 358 home runs, a lifetime .285 batting average, 1,430 RBI's, 2,120 games played, all this for a man who spent most of his career crouching behind home plate wearing the tools of ignorance, as a catcher's equipment is known. A look at the all-time leaders will find Lawrence Peter Berra, better known as Yogi, second among catchers in lifetime home runs, and first in consecutive games as a catcher without an error (148) and consecutive chances as a catcher without an error (950). A check of all-time World Series records will find Yogi first in number of World Series (14), number of World Series victories (10), number of World Series games (75), number of at-bats (259), and number of hits (71). Yogi won three Most Valuable Player awards (1951, 1954, 1955) and is one of only six men to have managed pennant winners in both leagues (1964 Yankees, 1973 Mets). In 1972 Yogi Berra was inducted into the Baseball Hall of Fame.

Yogi is a member of an even more exclusive club than the Baseball Hall of Fame. He is one of only a handful of mortals who has his own syntactical pattern, known as the Berraism in baseball lexicon. Commenting on baseball Yogi said, "Ninety percent of the game is half mental." When asked why he no longer went to a popular restaurant, Yogi responded, "Nobody goes there anymore. It's too crowded." Explaining to a sportswriter upset over a bill of $8.95 for a breakfast of orange juice, coffee, and an English muffin, Yogi remarked, "That's because they have to import those English muffins." When

LISTENER'S GUIDE
to the B-flat Major Fugue
WELL-TEMPERED CLAVIER
Book One

PRELUDE

Pretty fast, pretty fast indeed.

VOICES

3

MAJOR FEATURES

Very happy subject.
Two ultraconsistent countersubjects.

SPECIAL DEVICE

Both episodes are sequential.

FORM

First entry in the soprano; second entry in the alto; third entry in the bass; fourth entry in the soprano; first episode; fifth entry in the alto in minor; sixth entry in the bass in minor; second episode, fake entry of the subject in the alto; seventh entry in the soprano in major; eighth entry in the alto in major; coda.

---

asked for the correct time, Yogi queried, "Now?" When asked by sportswriters in August 1973 whether his then last-place Mets had any chance to win the pennant, Yogi declared, "It ain't over till it's over."

The number of Berraisms has grown exponentially over the years as others besides Yogi have realized their charm and begun to invent their own. Because of the multiplicity of Berraisms, it is now often difficult to ascertain which were uttered by Yogi himself. Since the list of Berraisms is already so long, it can't get any longer, I don't think Yogi would mind one more Berraism, this one concerning this fugue, B-flat Major. "The form of the B-flat Major fugue Book One is so simple, I can't follow it."

This fugue is 48 measures long, 32 of which are the four-measure subject, which runs eight times. Two ultraconsistent countersubjects run each time against the subject. So 32 out of 48 measures in this fugue (67 percent) are just the subject running and the two countersubjects running in different permutations of voices. The wonder of this fugue, to explain our Berraism, is that while listening to it we don't notice that last fact.

This fugue has the happiest and most joyous subject in the *Well-Tempered*. On the strength of its joyful subject, B-flat Major Book One makes it into the Top Ten.

b–flat minor

BOOK ONE

THIS FUGUE is written in an OLD STYLE. Five-voice pieces were common in the century before Bach, but by Bach's time (and through to the present) few pieces used more than four voices. Also, this fugue is written in $\frac{2}{2}$, a common time signature before Bach, but already replaced in Bach's time by $\frac{4}{4}$ as the dominant time signature. The order of entries for this fugue — highest to lowest — was very common before Bach. Finally, notice the simple, on-the-beat "square" rhythms of this fugue. Simple, straightforward rhythms were common before Bach.

This is the only fugue in the *Well-Tempered* that starts strettoing two thirds of the way through and intensifies the stretto as the fugue progresses to its end. The first stretto appears with entry 13 in the fiftieth measure of this 75-measure fugue. Entries 13 and 14 run in stretto separated by one measure. After entry 15, the stretto intensifies as entries 16 in soprano II and 17 in the alto overlap completely.

Finally, after an intervening episode, the stretto in the fugue and the fugue itself culminate with a REEXPOSITION IN STRETTO (entries 18–22). All five voices have entries of the subject in stretto in the same highest to lowest (soprano I to bass) order of entries as in the exposition.

LISTENER'S GUIDE
to the b-flat minor Fugue
WELL-TEMPERED CLAVIER
Book One

PRELUDE

Expressive chords.

VOICES

5 (from highest to lowest): soprano I, soprano II, alto, tenor, bass.

MAJOR FEATURE

This fugue is written in an old style (old for Bach). See the essay for more on old-style fugues.

SPECIAL DEVICE

Stretto. This is a fugue that uses stretto.

Reexposition in stretto — entries 18–22.

FORM

First entry in soprano I; second entry in soprano II; very long codetta; third entry in the alto; fourth entry in the tenor; short codetta; fifth entry in the bass; first episode; sixth entry in soprano I in major; seventh entry in soprano II in minor; eighth entry in the tenor; one measure; ninth entry in the bass; second episode; tenth entry in the alto in major; third episode; eleventh entry in soprano II in minor; twelfth entry in the bass; thirteenth entry in soprano I, fourteenth entry in soprano II in stretto; fifteenth entry in the tenor; sixteenth entry in soprano II and seventeenth entry in the alto overlapping completely; fourth episode; eighteenth entry in soprano I, nineteenth entry in soprano II in stretto, twentieth entry in the alto in stretto, twenty-first entry in the tenor in stretto, twenty-second entry in the bass in stretto; coda.

LISTENING HINTS

1. Very short subject.

2. The subject of this fugue is hard to hear and follow, so listen closely.

3. The first codetta is much longer than the subject.

4. Entries 16 and 17 overlap completely.

5. Entries 18–22 are a reexposition in stretto. All five voices have the subject successively in stretto from the highest voice — soprano I — to the lowest voice — the bass.

B Major

BOOK ONE

WHAT DOES this fugue have in common with C Major Book One, c-sharp minor Book One, d-sharp minor Book One, f-sharp minor Book One, a minor Book One, B-flat Major Book One, c minor Book Two, and E-flat Major Book Two?

They are all members of my Two-Thirds Club — single fugues two thirds or more of which are occupied by entries of their subject. There are nine fugues in the Two-Thirds Club, slightly more than one out of every six fugues in the *Well-Tempered*. Twenty-seven of the 48 fugues in the *Well-Tempered* are at least 50 percent occupied by entries of their subject. (These statistics include only the first subject of fugues. If we included entries of second and third subjects, the Two-Thirds Club and the Over 50 Percent Club would be even larger.)

These figures illustrate a crucial principle of Bach's fugues: the subject is the star. Bach often uses many entries of the subject to ensure that it *is* the star, in spite of the lurking danger that if *too* many entries are used, the audience will become indifferent to the subject. To prevent that, Bach avails himself of a great variety of large-level devices and techniques in the Two Thirds Club fugues.

C Major Book One is a stretto fugue. D-sharp minor Book One, a minor Book One, c minor Book Two, and E-flat Major Book Two are fugues that use stretto. F-sharp minor Book One is a double fugue. C-sharp minor Book One is a triple fugue. B-flat Major Book One employs two ultraconsistent countersubjects. B Major Book One has

LISTENER'S GUIDE
to the B Major Fugue
WELL–TEMPERED CLAVIER
Book One

PRELUDE

Short compared with the fugue.

VOICES

4

MAJOR FEATURE

Many entries and only three episodes.

SPECIAL DEVICES

Stretto. This is a fugue that hardly uses stretto at all. The only two entries in stretto, 8 and 9, overlap by only two notes.

Counterexposition. entries 7–10.

FORM

First entry in the tenor; second entry in the alto; third entry in the soprano; fourth entry in the bass; first episode; fifth entry in the tenor; second episode; sixth entry in the alto; seventh entry in the soprano in inversion; eighth entry in the alto in inversion, ninth entry in the bass in stretto overlapping with the eighth entry by the tiniest amount; half a measure; tenth entry in the tenor; third episode; eleventh entry in the alto; twelfth and last entry in the soprano; coda.

LISTENING HINT

The last note of the subject, often trilled, is a recognizable feature of the subject.

the simplest overall structure of the fugues in the Two-Thirds Club. Even so, it has a counterexposition (entries 7–10), and the tiniest bit of stretto between entries 8 and 9.

The first three notes of the subject of this fugue are very similar to the first three notes of the subject of B-flat Major Book One. Every time I hear the first three notes of this fugue, I expect to hear B-flat Major Book One.

b minor
BOOK ONE

NO MATTER how many times I listen to it, no matter how many times I study it, no matter how many more times I listen to this fugue, whenever I think about b minor Book One the same three thoughts come to mind: this fugue is long; this fugue is slow; this fugue is not one of my favorites. Bach wrote the word *largo* at the beginning of this fugue to indicate to performers that it should be played at a very slow speed, or TEMPO, and boy, did he mean it!

I have formed the Long, Slow, and Not My Favorite Club of fugues from the *Well-Tempered,* and this fugue is a charter member. Why? After all, Bach is usually the master of endings. Unlike Beethoven and his *48 consecutive* C Major chords at the end of the last movement of his Fifth Symphony, Bach usually knew exactly how to end a piece or a collection of pieces in an utterly organic way. What happened in this fugue? Did Bach somehow fall asleep at the switch at the end of Book One of the *Well-Tempered?* Our answer to this question lies in the subject of this fugue, as answers to our questions about fugues so often do.

As we discussed in "What Is the *Well-Tempered Clavier?*" there are 12 different notes in an octave. The subject of this fugue uses all of the notes, seven from its own key and five borrowed, or taken, from another key. This is quite remarkable. Most fugues in the *Well-Tempered* use only notes from their own key, or possibly one or two borrowed notes in addition.

The fact that the subject of this fugue uses all 12 pitches is often taken as evidence that this fugue belongs to a genre of music known

LISTENER'S GUIDE
to the b minor Fugue
WELL-TEMPERED CLAVIER
Book One

PRELUDE

Somewhat faster and livelier than the fugue.

VOICES

4

MAJOR FEATURES

Length, slowness.

SPECIAL DEVICES

All six episodes are canonic.

The material in the first, second, and sixth episodes is similar, and the third and fourth episodes use similar material.

FORM

First entry in the alto; second entry in the tenor; first codetta; third entry in the bass; second codetta; fourth entry in the soprano; first episode; fifth entry in the alto; second episode; sixth entry in the tenor; third episode; seventh entry in the bass; fourth episode; eighth entry in the tenor; ninth entry in the bass; fifth episode; tenth entry in the tenor; half a measure; eleventh entry in the bass; twelfth entry in the tenor; sixth episode; thirteenth entry in the bass; one measure; fourteenth entry (only half an entry) in the alto; coda.

---

as twelve-tone music. TWELVE-TONE MUSIC was pioneered in the twentieth century by the Viennese composer Arnold Schoenberg (1874–1951), and his two most famous students, Anton Webern (1883–1945) and Alban Berg (1885–1935). A twelve-tone piece makes extensive use of a structure known as a tone row. A TONE ROW is simply an arrangement of all twelve pitches in some order with no repetitions. Twelve-tone pieces use the tone row of the piece in many places and ways, and also use inversions, retrogrades, augmentations, and diminutions of the tone row. Twelve-tone music, with its use of the tone row to define and determine the structure of the smallest level of detail of pieces, differs sharply from music of prior centuries, which used various chord sequences, or CHORD PROGRESSIONS, to determine the structure of a piece on the smallest level of detail.

For two critical and obvious reasons it is clear that this fugue is *not* a twelve-tone piece.

First, this fugue has no tone row. The subject uses two C's, two C-sharps, two D's, three B's, and three F-sharp's before having one G-sharp or one A — not exactly the behavior of a tone row.

And second, although the subject of this fugue uses all 12 notes, nowhere else in the fugue (for example, in the episodes) does Bach put all 12 notes to use, as would be common in a twelve-tone piece.

Thus our answer to the question of whether this fugue is a twelve-tone piece is a resounding no. However, the fact that the subject of this fugue uses all 12 pitches does give us the key clue to understanding why this fugue is so long, slow, and not my favorite.

What better way, apparently, to end a collection of pieces, one in every key, than with a piece whose *theme* uses every pitch? The trouble is that once Bach decided to use a subject with all 12 pitches, he was forced to use a subject with a very slow tempo. That's because the borrowed notes and the chords that accompany those notes will sound silly, inane, or just plain wrong unless the subject moves slowly enough for our ears to adjust to the unusual and ever-changing harmonies. The slow tempo of the subject forced upon Bach by his decision to use a subject employing all 12 pitches, and thus the slow tempo for the whole fugue, as well as the complex harmonies forced upon Bach by all those borrowed notes in the subject, all give this fugue its long, slow, and not my favorite character.

A generation later, when Bach completed Book Two, he reconsidered the spirit with which to end a book of the *Well-Tempered Clavier,* and wrote a Bach-like ending for the final fugue of Book Two.

Thus ends Book One of the *Well-Tempered Clavier,* not with a bang but a whimper.

PART THREE

The WELL–TEMPERED CLAVIER

BOOK TWO

Introduction

SINCE BOOK TWO of the *Well-Tempered Clavier* was written approximately twenty years after Book One, we might expect to find large differences between the pieces in the two books. In particular, we might expect to find evidence of twenty years of maturation. The early and the late Mozart symphonies and Beethoven string quartets exhibit significant differences attributable to maturation. But when we put Book One and Book Two of the *Well-Tempered* side by side, we don't find the kind of obvious differences we might expect. I seriously doubt whether someone hearing a particular fugue from the *Well-Tempered* for the first time would be able to tell from which book it came.

The lack of such differences between Book One and Book Two is evidence of the fact that Bach formulated his compositional method early in his life and never needed to deviate substantially from it. But small differences do exist between Book One and Book Two.

Book One may be the tiniest bit freer and looser than Book Two. Book One contains two five-voice fugues and one two-voice fugue, while all the fugues in Book Two are for three or four voices. There is also the sprawling a minor fugue in Book One, the likes of which we do not find in Book Two.

On the other hand, 22 of the 26 three-voice fugues in the *Well-Tempered* have the last entry in their exposition in the bass, with all four exceptions in Book Two. Also, no fugue in Book One has a disappearing subject as does C-sharp Major Book Two.

One apparent difference between Book One and Book Two concerns performance time. Depending on the recording, it takes about 30 to 40 minutes longer to play Book Two than Book One. It is tempting to use this as evidence that in Book Two an older and more mature Bach is expounding his style more thoroughly.

As we examine the performance data more carefully, though, that apparent difference between Book One and Book Two breaks down. First, the fugues in Book Two take just about as much time to perform as the fugues in Book One. On the recording I used, for example, it takes about 65 minutes for the performance of Book One fugues, and the same amount of time for the performance of those in Book Two. So the difference in total performance time between the books is due almost entirely to the preludes. Here, too, the difference is not quite as telling as it might seem at first. Part of the performance-time difference between Book One and Book Two arises simply from repetitions of sections of some of the preludes from Book Two: ten of the preludes in Book Two contain repeated sections, while only one prelude in Book One has a repeated section.

While the differences between Book One and Book Two are not great, there is one interesting similarity. In the first fugue of both books of the *Well-Tempered*, Bach has left his signature. Remember our alphabetical code (A = 1, B = 2, and so on). So B-A-C-H is 14 and J-S-B-A-C-H is 41. The subject of the first fugue in Book One, C Major, has 14 notes, and Bach makes prominent and important use of the fourteenth entry of the subject of this fugue. In C Major Book Two, Bach leaves his signature in measure 41 by means of the omission of one sixteenth note.

C Major

BOOK TWO

THIS FUGUE belongs to a group I call simple fugues. SIMPLE FUGUES aren't double or triple fugues, don't have stretto, and don't have entries in inversion. In a simple fugue, the major units of composition, episodes and entries, are distinct and easy to hear, even the first time you listen to the piece.

Simple Fugues in the *Well-Tempered Clavier*

Book One	*Book Two*
c minor	C Major
E flat Major	f minor
B-flat Major	b minor

Four of these — this fugue, C Major Book Two, c minor Book One, f minor Book Two, and E-flat Major Book One — form a family. For more about them and their relationships, see the essay at the f minor fugue Book Two.

The structure of this fugue is easy enough to follow: a subject you can't miss, only four episodes, all sequential, each wrought very obviously from the head of the subject. Episodes 1, 2, and 4 are sequential and canonic, and the fourth and last episode starts out just like the first but continues on to be a double episode.

And although this fugue is one of only two in the *Well-Tempered* that doesn't have a last entry (D Major Book One is the other one), its

LISTENER'S GUIDE
to the C Major Fugue
WELL-TEMPERED CLAVIER
Book Two

PRELUDE

Begins with a firm C in the bass, announcing that the *Well-Tempered* has returned.

VOICES

3

MAJOR FEATURES

A member of the Superstar Four.
Sequential canonic episodes.
No last entry.

SPECIAL DEVICE

Double episodes. The second and fourth episodes are double. The fourth episode starts out just like the first episode, but then it breaks differently from the first episode and runs to twice the length of the first episode.

FORM

First entry in the alto; second entry in the soprano; third entry in the bass; first episode, sequential and canonic; fourth entry in the alto in minor; fifth entry in the soprano in minor; second episode, sequential; sixth entry in the bass in major; third episode, sequential; seventh entry in the alto; eighth entry in the soprano; fourth episode, a double episode, starts out sounding just like the first episode, but then it breaks differently from the first episode and continues on to twice the length of the first episode; end section: a figure built from the first part of the subject runs in each voice, first in the bass, next in the alto, finally in the soprano; coda.

LISTENING HINTS

1. Listen closely to the end section; there is no last entry.
2. All the episodes in this fugue are sequential.
3. The first episode and both parts of the double fourth episode are sequential and canonic. The canon is always between the soprano and alto with the bass free.

---

end section is clear and easy to follow. The last 16 measures are divided into four groups of four. In the first three groups each voice, from bass to soprano, takes a turn having a four-measure phrase consisting of the first two measures of the subject run twice in sequence, the second time a step lower than the first. So in the end section Bach does not use a last entry but, nevertheless, is able to retain the length of the subject, four measures, by substituting a repetition of the first half of the subject, one step lower, for the second half of the subject. The last four measures are the coda.

The best things about this fugue are the first, second, and fourth episodes. (The first and fourth make the Top Ten Episodes.) All three are sequential and canonic, and they all are built from the first half of the subject in the upper voices and the second half of the subject in the lower voices. The second and fourth episodes are double episodes.

Let's take a closer look at two of the episodes in this fugue.

The eight-measure *first episode* is a classic sequential canonic episode. (See this fugue's cousin, c minor Book One, for more on classic sequential canonic episodes.) The canon is between the soprano and alto with the bass free. The two-measure sequence is built from both halves of the subject. The soprano and alto, in canon, use material from the head of the subject; the bass uses material from the second half of the subject. The two-measure sequence runs twice and starts to run a third time before breaking. The remaining measures of the episode help the fugue move to minor for the fourth entry.

At 12 measures the *fourth episode* is the longest in this fugue. It is also a double episode, being both twice as long as most of the episodes in this fugue and having two sequences, not one. The fourth episode starts out with the same two-measure sequence unit as the first episode. This time the sequence unit runs three times and starts to run a fourth time before breaking. The fourth episode breaks differently from the first episode, continues on to another sequence, and runs to twice the length of the first episode. In the seventh measure of this last episode Bach breaks the first sequence and begins the second sequence using syncopation.

Wanted! One sixteenth note named J. S. Bach, measure 41, in any voice.

Our hunt for the missing sixteenth begins with the eighth-note rest in the subject. The rest divides the two halves of the subject. The first half, consisting of six notes, slows from sixteenths, the fastest notes used in this fugue, to eighths, to quarters, to nothing, a rest, while the second half is all sixteenths. The rest in this fugue, like the rest in the E-flat Major fugue Book Two, is a pause, a breath, before the subject moves on.

It always seemed to me, especially when I was jumping rope to the *Well-Tempered* to get in shape for crew, that the action of the fugue was suspended for an instant during the rest in the subject. It was as if the rest wanted to extend the tiniest bit before and after where it belonged. This seemed to be especially true during entries in the bass. Then I noticed that during the sixth entry in the bass there was one sixteenth note "missing" during the rest in the subject.

Let me explain what I mean by "missing." This fugue is written in $\frac{2}{4}$ time, which means that every measure has two quarter notes. The fastest notes in the fugue are sixteenths. That makes a maximum of eight sixteenths per measure, or a maximum of eight slots or holes to fill.

From measure 23 through the second to last measure of the fugue, measure 81, each hole is filled in every measure except in measure 41. When I first noticed the missing sixteenth during the rest in the sixth entry of the subject, it confirmed my suspicion that the rest sounded ever so slightly longer than an eighth note. With all the voices not playing during the rest, the rest can get away with being longer than an eighth. However, I couldn't figure out why it was only this entry that was missing a sixteenth. The missing sixteenth sounded good enough; why had Bach used it only once? I wondered, that is, until I noticed that the sixteenth was missing from measure 41.

Forty-one, remember, is the sum of the value of the letters in J. S. Bach. Thus, the sixteenth is missing from measure J-S-B-A-C-H.

c minor

BOOK TWO

THERE ARE four voices in this fugue, but, curiously, the fourth voice, the bass, doesn't enter until two thirds of the way through the fugue. This is very strange. Bach does nothing like it anywhere else in the *Well-Tempered*. When the bass does finally come in, it has three entries in a row (entries 16–18). Entry 16 is the subject in augmentation and entry 17 is the melodic inversion of the subject. The entry of the bass actually divides the third section of this fugue into two parts. The first part of the third section (entries 8–15) has a lot of stretto, and the second part of the third section (the three bass entries, entries 16–18) has no stretto at all.

I don't know why Bach doesn't have the bass enter until two thirds of the way through, but I do know that in another fugue, C Major Organ Fugue (BWV 547), he does almost exactly the same thing. The C Major Organ Fugue has five voices, but the fifth voice, in the bass, doesn't enter until 68 percent of the way through. Like this fugue, the C Major Organ Fugue also uses stretto increasingly in each section. Clearly, c minor Book Two and the C Major Organ Fugue were cast from the same mold.

LISTENER'S GUIDE
to the c minor Fugue
WELL-TEMPERED CLAVIER
Book Two

PRELUDE

Just barely misses my Top Ten Preludes. Notice how the two voices alternate slow notes and fast notes.

VOICES

4. The bass does not enter until entry 16, so that for its first 18 measures (out of 28 total) this fugue is a three-voice fugue.

MAJOR FEATURE

Stretto

SPECIAL DEVICES:

Stretto. This is a fugue that uses stretto.

Augmentation.

Inversion.

NOTE

This fugue has five sections: The first section, exposition entries 1–3, has no stretto. The second section, entries 4–7, has no stretto. The third section, entries 8–18, has some stretto. The fourth section, entries 19–24, has even more stretto. The fifth and last section, the coda, has no stretto.

FORM

First section: first entry in the alto; second entry in the soprano; codetta; third entry in the tenor.

Second section: one measure; fake entry in the tenor; fake entry in the alto; fourth entry in the tenor in major; fifth entry in the soprano; one measure; sixth entry in the alto in major; seventh entry in the tenor in major; one and a half measures.

Third section: eighth entry in the soprano in minor, ninth entry in the alto in stretto in augmentation, tenth entry in the tenor in stretto in inversion; eleventh entry in the alto, twelfth entry in the soprano in stretto, thirteenth entry in the tenor in stretto in major, fourteenth entry in the soprano in stretto in major, fifteenth entry in the alto in stretto in major; sixteenth entry in the bass in augmentation (this is the first entry for the bass); seventeenth entry in the bass in inversion; eighteenth entry in the bass in major; half a measure.

Fourth section: nineteenth entry in the alto in minor, twentieth entry in the soprano in stretto; twenty-first entry in the soprano in major, twenty-second entry in the alto in stretto, twenty-third entry in the tenor in stretto in major, twenty-fourth entry in the bass in stretto in inversion.

Fifth section: coda.

LISTENING HINTS

1. Beware of the two fake entries before the fourth entry.

2. There isn't much of a break between the exposition and the second section. However, the breaks between the second and third sections, the third and fourth sections, and the fourth and fifth sections are extremely clear.

C–sharp Major

BOOK TWO

WHERE, OH, where has the second half of the subject gone? Where, oh, where can it be? Or was it ever there in the first place?

Because it is the main attraction, we usually begin our discussion of a fugue with its subject. For this fugue, I have a problem: I'm not sure how long the subject of this fugue is. There are two possibilities:

1. The subject is only four notes long. These four notes, all of them, are eighth notes, making the four-note version of the subject of this fugue only *half* a measure, by far the shortest subject in the *Well-Tempered*. Not only is it short, it feels short, indicating that maybe the subject is longer than four notes. On the other hand, there are 37 entries of the four-note version of the subject, by far the most of any subject in the *Well-Tempered*.

2. The subject is 12 notes long, the four notes of the four-note version plus another eight notes. The trouble with this option is that there are only seven entries of the 12-note version, three in the exposition (entries 1–3), three more in the middle of the fugue (entries 21, 23, 24), and one other (entry 5). In the Listener's Guide I have listed all 44 entries of both versions of the subject together and marked the entries of the 12-note version of the subject with an asterisk (*).

The last entry (entry 24) of the 12-note version finishes too early — in the sixteenth measure of this 35-measure fugue. So if the subject of this fugue does have 12 notes, that version does a pretty good disappearing act in the last two thirds of the piece, and isn't even present that much in the first third.

LISTENER'S GUIDE
to the C-sharp Major Fugue
WELL-TEMPERED CLAVIER
Book Two

PRELUDE

This prelude is divided into two sections. The first section is in $\frac{4}{4}$ at a moderate tempo. The second section is in $\frac{3}{8}$ at a faster tempo.

VOICES

3

MAJOR FEATURE

4-note subject or 12-note subject? See the essay.

SPECIAL DEVICES

Entries of the subject in melodic inversion, augmentation, and diminution.

Stretto. This is a fugue that uses stretto.

NOTES

1. In the exposition, entries come in after only four notes.

2. Entries marked with an asterisk are the 12-note version of the subject. Unmarked entries are the 4-note version of the subject.

FORM

First entry* in the bass; second entry* in the soprano; third entry* in the alto in inversion; fourth entry in the bass in inversion; fifth entry* in the soprano; sixth entry in the alto; seventh entry in the bass; eighth entry in the soprano in diminution; ninth entry in the alto in diminution; tenth entry in the bass in diminution in inversion; half a measure; eleventh entry in the bass; twelfth entry in the alto; thirteenth entry in the soprano; one measure; fourteenth entry in the bass in inversion, fifteenth entry in the soprano in stretto in inversion, sixteenth entry in the soprano in stretto in inversion; one measure; seventeenth entry in the bass in inversion, eighteenth entry in the soprano in stretto in inversion, nineteenth entry in the alto in stretto, twentieth entry in the bass in inversion; two and a half measures; twenty-first entry* in the bass, twenty-second entry in the soprano in stretto in inversion, twenty-third entry* in the alto in stretto in inversion; twenty-fourth entry* in the soprano in inversion; one measure; twenty-fifth entry in the bass; one measure; twenty-sixth entry in the alto in diminution in inversion; twenty-seventh entry in the bass in diminution in inversion; twenty-eighth entry in the alto in diminution in inversion; twenty-ninth entry in the bass in diminution; two measures; thirtieth entry in the bass in diminution in inversion; thirty-first entry in the soprano in diminution; one and a half measures; thirty-second entry in the bass; half a measure; thirty-third entry in the soprano in inversion; thirty-fourth entry in the bass; thirty-fifth entry in the bass in inversion; thirty-sixth entry in the bass in inversion; thirty-seventh entry in the bass in augmentation; thirty-eighth entry in the soprano in inversion; thirty-ninth entry in the soprano; one measure; fortieth entry in the alto in inversion; forty-first entry in the alto in inversion; forty-second entry in the alto in inversion; forty-third entry in the bass; two and a half measures; forty-fourth and last entry in the soprano in diminution; coda.

LISTENING HINTS

1. Remember that the subject is very short, probably only 4 notes.

2. Despite the large number of entries in this fugue — the most entries of any fugue in the *Well-Tempered* — it really isn't that hard to follow.

3. In case you get lost, good places to catch up are the eleventh entry in the bass, the fourteenth entry in the bass in inversion, the twenty-first entry in the bass, and entries 34–37 in the bass.

4. The last entry of this fugue, entry 44, may be difficult to hear, as Bach adds an extra voice at the end of the fugue.

So what happens to the last eight notes of the subject? Where do they go? Or were they ever there at all?

Usually, Bach does not alter the subject at all during a fugue, just as you wouldn't alter the foundation of your house once you had started to build over it. Occasionally, to fit the subject into the middle section of a fugue, Bach will change the length of the last note or two of the subject or change the last interval of the subject. But never in the *Well-Tempered* or the organ fugues does Bach alter the subject nearly as drastically as in this fugue.

So we have two choices. We can conclude that the subject of this fugue is 12 notes long, eight notes of which disappear in the last two thirds of the fugue; or that the subject is only four notes long and the extra eight notes that show up in seven entries are not part of the subject but are something else. But it's just not like Bach to let two thirds of the foundation of a piece slip away. Besides, there doesn't seem to be anything too special about the seven entries of the 12-note version of the subject. Why not six entries? Or eight?

If the last of the seven entries of the 12-note version of the subject came somewhat later in the fugue, say two thirds of the way through rather than one third, I would be strongly tempted to say that the subject of this fugue has 12 notes. For example, D Major Book One has no entry of the subject in the last 10 of a 26-measure total (38 percent).

Another factor weighing in against the 12-note version of the subject is stretto in the fugue's exposition. If the subject is indeed 12 notes, then this fugue has stretto in its exposition, the entries in the exposition coming in after only four notes. Only one other fugue in the *Well-Tempered,* D Major Book Two, has stretto in its exposition. Usually, Bach stays away from stretto in the exposition so the audience won't be confused about the most basic structural point of the fugue — how many voices there are — and remain so for the rest of the fugue.

This leads us to conclude that the subject of this fugue is four notes long. The four-note version of the subject is quite respectable: 44 entries, entries in inversion, augmentation, diminution, and stretto. But we'd have a little explaining to do about the eight extra notes that occur in seven entries of the subject.

There is one additional piece of evidence strongly bolstering the idea that the subject of this fugue has four notes. At half a measure, the four-note version of the subject is the shortest *first* subject in the *Well-Tempered,* but not the shortest subject. The second subject of F-sharp Major Book One is also only half a measure. There are other similarities between the two subjects:

1. Both this fugue and F-sharp Major Book One are three-voice fugues.

2. In the exposition of both the subject of this fugue and the second subject in F-sharp Major Book One, the last of the three voices to enter is the alto.

3. In both this fugue and the second subject of F-sharp Major Book One, the alto enters with the melodic inversion of the subject. These are the only two subjects in the *Well-Tempered* whose exposition uses the melodic inversion, or indeed any variation, of the subject.

Four-note version or 12-note version, all obvious traces of the subject are pretty much gone by the end of the fugue. At the end Bach adds an extra voice and has lots of fast runs and chords in the now four voices. It's as if by the end of the fugue Bach might be trying to lose the subject entirely.

c–sharp minor

BOOK TWO

AS WE know, in a double fugue, the two subjects are either exposed separately and combine later, or the second subject always accompanies the first subject. The differences between the two kinds may even outweigh their similarity of having two subjects. In the type with two subjects exposed separately, the second subject is free to roam through the entire fugue, interlocking with the first subject as frequently or infrequently as it pleases. For example, in this fugue, after its own exposition the second subject never really combines at all with the first subject. In the type in which the second subject always runs against the first subject, the placement of entries of the second subject is restricted to those of the first subject.

In nine of the ten double and triple fugues in the *Well-Tempered*, the second and third subjects are very different from the first subject and bear no obvious or audible relation to it. The one exception is this fugue, c-sharp minor Book Two. Not only is the second subject similar to the first, it is taken directly from the first subject — specifically, from the second part of the first subject. The first subject of this fugue is made up of six groups of triplets. The second subject of this fugue is just the last two groups of triplets repeated one, two, three, or more times.

We cannot help noticing the similarity between the head of the first subject of this fugue and the head of the subject of d minor Book Two. Both subjects begin with four groups of triplets. Both subjects diverge after the four groups of triplets. The second half of the subject

LISTENER'S GUIDE
to the c-sharp minor Fugue
WELL-TEMPERED CLAVIER
Book Two

PRELUDE

A slow and emotional soprano aria.

VOICES

3

MAJOR FEATURE

Double fugue. The second subject of the fugue is built directly from the second half of the first subject.

SPECIAL DEVICES

Double fugue.
Melodic inversion.

NOTE

Because Bach uses the second subject in a much looser way than the first, and because there are so many different entries of the short second subject, I will not list specific entries but only write "second subject" to indicate them. So that you don't get confused, be warned that sometimes there are many entries of the second subject, and that sometimes the material from the second subject can sound episodic. However, trying to follow this fugue is not hopeless, as most entries of the first subject, especially the ascending stepwise scale at its beginning, stand out.

FORM

First entry of the first subject in the bass; second entry of the first subject in the soprano; codetta, second subject; third entry of the first subject in the alto; first episode, many entries of the second subject; fourth entry of the first subject in the soprano; fifth entry of the first subject in the alto; one measure, second subject; sixth entry of the first subject in the bass in major; second episode, second subject; seventh entry of the first subject in the soprano in inversion; eighth entry of the first subject in the alto in inversion; ninth entry of the first subject in the bass in inversion; tenth entry of the first subject in the alto; third episode: many entries of the second subject; eleventh entry of the first subject in the soprano; fourth episode, second subject; twelfth entry of the first subject in the alto in inversion; thirteenth entry of the first subject in the bass; fifth episode, second subject; fourteenth entry of the first subject in the alto; sixth episode, second subject; fifteenth entry of the first subject in the alto; sixteenth entry of the first subject in the bass; coda.

of d minor Book Two is very simple: a slow, stepwise, descending, chromatic scale. The second half of the subject of this fugue is more complex: two additional groups of triplets.

The complexity of this fugue and the lack of complexity of d minor Book Two are related to the degree of complexity of the second half of their subjects. D minor Book Two is quite a simple fugue, highlighting the simple second half of its subject. C-sharp minor Book Two is complex, as it builds the second subject from the complex second half of its first subject.

D Major

BOOK TWO

DA, DA, da, daaah; short, short, short, long — the beginning of Beethoven's Fifth Symphony, you say? Actually, it's the beginning of this fugue. Beethoven, a great fan of the *Well-Tempered*, played it often. Much of Beethoven's earliest fame came as a result of rave reviews for his performances of the *Well-Tempered*. My feeling is that Beethoven got the idea for the wonderful theme of his Fifth Symphony from the subject of this fugue, but I can't offer any proof. Everyone I know disagrees with me, pointing out that many other pieces use a short, short, short, long motive.

This is the only fugue in the *Well-Tempered* that strettos during its exposition: entries 3 and 4 of this four-voice fugue run in stretto. Usually, Bach stays away from stretto in the exposition because it could hopelessly confuse the audience for the rest of the fugue. The audience may not be able to tell when the exposition is over and the middle section has begun and thus might not even be able to tell how many voices the fugue has. The danger of confusion is even greater in an already complex stretto fugue. So we should be a bit surprised that Bach chose a stretto fugue to use stretto in the exposition.

The danger, however, is somewhat mitigated in this fugue by the fact that the two entries in stretto in the exposition are in the bass and the soprano, the two easiest voices to hear and recognize, so we in the audience can most easily tell they haven't entered the fugue yet. When the bass and soprano run the subject in stretto, we can tell that it must still be the exposition and that the middle section hasn't started yet.

LISTENER'S GUIDE
to the D Major Fugue
WELL-TEMPERED CLAVIER
Book Two

PRELUDE

One of the longest in the *Well-Tempered.*

VOICES

4

MAJOR FEATURE

Stretto.

SPECIAL DEVICES

Stretto. This is a stretto fugue. Counterexposition in stretto (entries 21–24).

FORM

First entry in the tenor; second entry in the alto; codetta (short); third entry in the soprano, fourth entry in the bass in stretto; two and a half measures; fifth entry in the alto in minor; sixth entry in the soprano in minor; one measure; seventh entry in the alto, eighth entry in the soprano in stretto; five measures; ninth entry in the tenor in minor, tenth entry in the soprano in stretto in minor, eleventh entry in the alto in stretto in minor; one measure; twelfth entry in the bass in minor; one and a half measures; thirteenth entry in the bass in minor; fourteenth entry in the soprano in stretto, fifteenth entry in the alto in stretto; three and a half measures; sixteenth entry in the alto, seventeenth entry in the alto in stretto in minor, eighteenth entry in the soprano in stretto in major; five measures; nineteenth entry in the tenor; one and a half measures; twentieth entry in the bass in minor, fake entry in the tenor in stretto in minor; counterexposition in stretto: twenty-first entry in the soprano, twenty-second entry in the alto in stretto in minor, twenty-third entry in the tenor in stretto in major, twenty-fourth and last entry in the bass in stretto in minor; coda.

LISTENING HINT

You can't miss the three repeated notes at the beginning of the subject.

Bach's use of stretto in this fugue shows that he did not always feel compelled to follow rules about how a fugue should be written. On the other hand, Bach's avoidance of stretto in the exposition of the other 47 fugues in the *Well-Tempered* shows that he usually followed a rule when it helped make a wonderful piece.

d minor

BOOK TWO

THE TWO-PART subject of this fugue is like a roller coaster ride in reverse. First the subject storms upward, rising in four groups of fast triplets. Then the second half of the subject takes its sweet time heading downward, in one jump and then a scale descending slowly by step.

Because the descending notes are CHROMATIC NOTES, notes from another key, they may sound a bit strange. Every musical scale, major or minor, has seven notes. There are a total of 12 different pitches. For a piece written in a given key, seven of those 12 notes belong to the key and five do not.

But composers can still use notes that don't belong to a certain key. Composers often borrow notes from other keys, you might say, though they usually sound a bit foreign or strange. Bach didn't use the chromatic descending line much in the *Well-Tempered*, but overall it was one of his favorite ways to use chromatic notes. Nowhere in the *Well-Tempered* does Bach use the chromatic descending line in its full glory as he does in this fugue, via the contrast with the fast ascending triplets.

LISTENER'S GUIDE
to the d minor Fugue
WELL-TEMPERED CLAVIER
Book Two

PRELUDE

My friend Jon Wallenberger says this prelude sounds like a Vivaldi concerto. I like the way the soprano and bass switch off slow notes and fast notes in a manner similar to the C-sharp Major Prelude Book One. This prelude is also similar to the D Major and d minor preludes in Book One.

VOICES

3

MAJOR FEATURES

Triplets in the subject.
Chromatic notes in the subject.

SPECIAL DEVICES

Stretto. This is a fugue that uses stretto.

Melodic inversion.

FORM

First entry in the alto; second entry in the soprano; codetta; third entry in the bass; first episode; fake entry in the bass, fake entry in the soprano in stretto in inversion; fourth entry in the soprano; second episode; fifth entry in the alto, sixth entry in the soprano in stretto; third episode; seventh entry in the alto in inversion, eighth entry in the bass in stretto in inversion; ninth entry in the bass (this entry is a slightly abbreviated version of the subject); fourth episode (long); fake entry in the tenor; tenth and last entry in the soprano; coda.

E–flat Major
BOOK TWO

———

GET READY to sing! E-flat Major Book Two has the most singable subject in the *Well-Tempered,* and I love to sing it. On the strength of this fugue's wonderful subject, it's not only in my Top Ten Fugues, but also in my Superstar Four. The subject combined with a preponderance of long, slow notes make this an excellent piece for a chorus or choir.

The singable subject is just one feature of the old (for Bach) style in which this fugue is written, harking back to the centuries before Bach when most music was vocal. Its large-level structure, which includes three pairs of stretto entries, serves as a very simple frame on which to support the singable subject.

This fugue's six-measure subject is one of the longest in the *Well-Tempered.* There is a "seventh" measure that, though technically not part of the subject, always follows the six measures of the subject. This seventh measure also serves as a one-measure codetta between the second and third and the third and fourth entries. The subject is very slow getting started: the first measure contains just one long whole note, and the second measure a half note, a rest, and a quarter note. The last four measures of the subject move a lot faster.

Let's look more closely at the last four measures of the six-measure subject, and at the seventh measure that always follows: the third and fourth measures form a two-measure sequence unit that is repeated one step lower in the fifth and sixth measures of the subject. That's no big deal. What is a big deal is that the sixth measure is itself

LISTENER'S GUIDE
to the E-flat Major Fugue
WELL–TEMPERED CLAVIER
Book Two

PRELUDE

Near the end of this prelude Bach recaps its beginning.

VOICES

4

MAJOR FEATURE

A wonderful, singable subject, one of the best in the *Well-Tempered*.

SPECIAL DEVICE

Stretto. This is a fugue that uses stretto. There are three pairs of stretto entries — 5–6, 7–8, and 10–11.

FORM

First entry in the bass; second entry in the tenor; one-measure codetta; third entry in the alto; one-measure codetta; fourth entry in the soprano; first episode; fifth entry in the tenor, sixth entry in the bass in stretto; one measure; seventh entry in the alto, eighth entry in the soprano in stretto; second episode (long); ninth entry in the tenor; tenth entry in the soprano, eleventh entry in the bass in stretto; coda.

LISTENING HINT

The two codettas and the first episode are very short. The second episode is very long.

a one-measure sequence unit repeated two steps lower in the seventh measure that always follows.

The question is: how should we hear the sixth measure of the subject? As part of the second run for the two-measure sequence unit (measures 3–4 and 5–6 of the subject)? Or as the first run for the one-measure sequence unit (measures 6 and "7" of the subject)?

No matter which way we hear the sixth measure, we will always miss hearing it the other way. Every time we hear this fugue we'll feel like we've missed something — because we really have — and we'll want to hear the fugue again. Of course, the next time we hear the fugue we'll also miss something, so we'll want to hear it again, and so on. The ambiguous sixth measure of the subject helps make this a piece to which we can listen again and again without getting bored.

Bach uses similar ambiguous notes in the C Major Two-Part Invention. See that Appendix for details.

d–sharp minor

BOOK TWO

TWO COUNTERSUBJECTS and only two episodes pretty much says it all about this fugue structurally. Twelve out of 16 entries are involved in the exposition or one of the two counterexpositions. Another two entries at the end of the fugue (entries 15 and 16) overlap completely, the entry in the tenor being the melodic inversion of the subject.

While this fugue's structure is quite simple, the harmonies are not. With the first five or six notes of the subject Bach establishes that the fugue is going to be slow, chromatic, and emotional. This fugue, with its 16 entries and 2 episodes, demonstrates Bach's remarkable ability to come up with numerous harmonies to run against the same theme. And in this fugue, unlike in other fugues (such as B-flat Major Book One) with many entries and only a couple of episodes, Bach does not rely on one or two countersubjects to run consistently against the subject.

The end section, entry 14 through the coda, is very interesting. Bach probably designed the subject of this fugue so that it could run against itself in inversion. The whole fugue, and especially the end section, builds to the last two entries, 15 and 16. Notice that during the fourteenth entry in the bass, the upper three voices alternate between short chords and rests, rather than the moving lines that accompany all the other entries of the subject. It seems that the upper three voices are taking a bit of a breath before driving through to the end of the fugue.

LISTENER'S GUIDE
to the d-sharp minor Fugue
WELL-TEMPERED CLAVIER
Book Two

PRELUDE

Reminds me of the c minor prelude Book Two. I like the trills and the move to major.

VOICES

4

MAJOR FEATURE

The three repeated notes at the beginning of the subject.

SPECIAL DEVICES

Stretto. This is a fugue that hardly uses stretto at all.

The last two entries overlap completely.

FORM

First entry in the alto; second entry in the tenor; codetta; third entry in the bass; fourth entry in the soprano; first episode; fifth entry in the bass; sixth entry in the alto; seventh entry in the tenor; eighth entry in the soprano; half a measure; ninth entry in the alto, fake entry in the tenor in stretto, tenth entry in the bass in stretto; eleventh entry in the soprano; twelfth entry in the alto; thirteenth entry in the tenor; second episode (long); fourteenth entry in the bass; one measure; fifteenth entry in the soprano simultaneously with the sixteenth entry in the tenor in inversion; coda.

LISTENING HINTS

1. This fugue has two counterexpositions: entries 5–8 and entries 10–13.

2. The second episode is long.

3. The last two entries overlap completely.

E Major
BOOK TWO

WHAT LINES! What gorgeous lines!

All the individual voices in this fugue — soprano, alto, tenor, and bass — have such wonderful parts, such wonderfully shaped lines. Try to follow a single part while you listen to the fugue. Specially recommended are the soprano and bass.

The subject of this fugue is very simple. The first half ascends with one step and one jump. The second half of the subject descends by step. It would certainly be an example of motivicness if Bach used a lot of short, stepwise ascending and descending scales. However, Bach does something more than adhere to the letter of motivicness. He follows what we might call the SPIRIT OF MOTIVICNESS. In the same spirit as the subject, Bach fills this fugue with ascending and descending stepwise lines — not just short lines, but long, wonderful long lines.

E Major Book Two works well for chorus or choir, as do E-flat Major Book Two and B Major Book Two. Bach wrote these three fugues in an older style, dating from the time when most music was vocal music.

Entries 13 through 17 run the subject in DIMINUTION — all the notes in the subject have their rhythmic values cut in half. This is the only fugue in the *Well-Tempered* that uses entries of the subject in diminution. While the original form of the subject uses whole notes and half notes, the diminuted form uses half notes and quarter notes.

LISTENER'S GUIDE
to the E Major Fugue
WELL-TEMPERED CLAVIER
Book Two

PRELUDE

This prelude, like nine others in Book Two, is divided into two sections, each of which is repeated. The music immediately before the repeat is excellent.

VOICES

4

MAJOR FEATURE

Each of the original parts — soprano, alto, tenor, bass — is wonderful.

SPECIAL DEVICES

Stretto. This is a fugue that uses stretto.

Counterexpositions. There are four: entries 5–8, entries 9–12, entries 13–16, and entries 19–22.

Diminution. Entries 13–17 are the diminution of the subject.

FORM

Exposition: first entry in the bass; second entry in the tenor; third entry in the alto; fourth entry in the soprano; first episode; first counterexposition: fifth entry in the alto, sixth entry in the tenor in stretto, seventh entry in the bass in stretto, eighth entry in the soprano in stretto; second episode; second counterexposition: ninth entry in the alto; tenth entry in the soprano in stretto; eleventh entry in the bass, twelfth entry in the tenor in stretto in minor; third episode; third counterexposition: thirteenth entry in the soprano in minor in diminution, fourteenth entry in the alto in stretto in minor in diminution; fifteenth entry in the tenor in diminution, sixteenth entry in the bass in stretto in minor in diminution; seventeenth entry in the bass in major in diminution, eighteenth entry in the alto in stretto; fourth episode; fourth counterexposition: nineteenth entry in the alto, twentieth entry in the tenor in stretto, twenty-first entry in the bass in stretto, twenty-second entry in the soprano in stretto; one measure; twenty-third and last entry in the bass; coda.

This fugue has four counterexpositions. Only a minor Book One and b-flat minor Book Two, the counterexposition kings of the *Well-Tempered* with five each, have more. All four counterexpositions in this fugue use stretto. In the third counterexposition all the entries are in diminution.

e minor
BOOK TWO

GREAT SUBJECT, great sequential canonic episodes, great move to major, great coda.

The subject of this fugue wins the award for the greatest variety of different note values. It uses triplets, quarter notes, groups of four sixteenth notes, and dotted-eighth-note/sixteenth-note combinations. In addition, the subject has some notes tied together, and other notes marked specially by Bach to be accented. This fugue is one of only four in the *Well-Tempered* with such accent marks. (D minor Book One, F Major Book Two, and a minor Book Two are the other three.)

The fugue comes to a complete stop twice at the end. In musical language such a stop is known as a FERMATA. This fugue is one of three in the *Well-Tempered* with a fermata. The others are a minor Book One and A-flat Major Book Two. The fermatas contribute to this fugue's powerful end section, which includes not only the coda, but also the first fermata, which comes before the ninth and last entry and the coda itself. Besides the second fermata, the coda contains sequences, a dramatic chord, and solos in the soprano and bass.

Given my enthusiastic treatment of this fugue, you might be wondering why it isn't in my Top Ten. Strictly personal here: I think that structurally this fugue is very similar to c minor Book One. But c minor Book One has and does everything this fugue has and does — a great subject, great sequential canonic episodes, a great move to major, and an awesome end section — in only 31 measures, while this fugue goes on for 86 measures. (Also I like c minor Book One's subject a little better.) There isn't room in my Top Ten for two such similar fugues.

LISTENER'S GUIDE
to the e minor Fugue
WELL-TEMPERED CLAVIER
Book Two

PRELUDE

Trill.

VOICES

3

MAJOR FEATURE

A subject that uses a wide and interesting variety of rhythms.

SPECIAL DEVICE

Sequential episode.

FORM

First entry in the soprano; second entry in the alto; third entry in the bass; first episode; fourth entry in the soprano in major; fifth entry in the alto in major; second episode; sixth entry in the bass in minor; third episode; seventh entry in the alto; fourth episode; eighth entry in the soprano; fifth episode, first fermata, more fifth episode; ninth and last entry in the bass; coda, second fermata, more coda.

LISTENING HINTS

1. The first episode is long and contains two sequences.

2. The third episode is short and contains one sequence.

3. The coda is long and includes a second fermata as well as solos in the soprano and bass.

Row, Row, Row Your Boat

Remember in elementary school singing ROUNDS — songs like "Row, Row, Row Your Boat," "Frère Jacques," and "Three Blind Mice" — in which one group started singing a melody and then another group came in with the same melody? Singing rounds gave us our first experience with IMITATIVE PIECES. Other kinds of imitative pieces are canons and fugues.

In a round, the first group of people to start singing are called, appropriately enough, the LEADERS and the next group to come in the FOLLOWERS. Some rounds have more than two groups of singers.

There is one important thing to remember about rounds: all the basic songs are very short. Rounds are a fun musical form and no doubt have been around as long as there have been elementary school teachers. Rounds are also very simple.

A close but slightly more complex relative of the round is the CANON. Canons, like rounds, start with one group leading and the other groups coming in as followers. The original canons were very much like rounds, with the leader and followers repeating the same melody over and over. As time progressed and canons, along with other kinds of pieces, got longer, they came to have music other than just the leading and following parts.

This development of canons is very similar to that of fugues, which also started out with all the parts chasing each other, and eventually evolved into pieces containing material other than just leading and following. By Bach's time, the other material in fugues far overtook in importance the chasing material.

Canons did not evolve as much. Even in Bach's time they still consisted of mostly leader and follower. But as they got longer, it was crucial that they contain other material. Here's why.

The power and wonder of a canon lie in the audience's somehow trying to listen to more than one moving voice at a time. But it is very difficult for the audience to do that for more than a short time. In an attempt to follow more than one voice, we in the audience try various strategies. We might listen to one voice and then quickly listen to the other voice, and then switch back to the first voice, and then to the second voice, and so on. Or we might try to follow only the rhythm in the two voices, or just the overall shape of the two voices. But after a short time, even these strategies don't work very well, and it becomes very hard to follow both voices taking part in the canon. Once we are unable simultaneously to follow both voices, the power of a canon is gone, and it loses its effectiveness.

So as canons got longer, they employed not only leading and following, but also OTHER SECTIONS with no leading and following. Rather than having one long section of leading and following, canons in the time of Bach had lots of little sections of leading and following, separated by other sections with no leading and following. Instead of giving up trying to follow one very long section of leading and following, the audience would try afresh every time to follow each of the short sections of leading and following.

The other sections in canons are much shorter and less important than the other sections in fugues. In canons, the leading and following sections remained by far the most important and longest sections. On the other hand, as fugues progressed through time, the other sections came to dominate the fugue almost to the point of excluding the fugue's following and chasing ancestry.

There are two ways that canons are important for the *Well-Tempered:*

Canonic Episodes. In many fugues from the *Well-Tempered* Bach has episodes that use tiny canons. These small CANONIC SECTIONS in episodes are especially effective because, as we have seen, canons are best in small doses. (See "Sequential Canonic Episodes" accompanying c minor Book One for more on the most important type of canonic episode.)

Perspective. Fugues themselves do not exist in a vacuum. Canons and rounds are among the types of pieces that use imitation. In particular, canons that contain some, but very little, other material help us put fugues with mostly other material into perspective.

F Major

BOOK TWO

ONE OF the inevitable tragedies of establishing a Baseball Hall of Fame or a list of Top Ten Fugues is that some great baseball players or wonderful fugues are going to be excluded.

Consider the great second baseman Nellie Fox. In his final year of Hall of Fame election eligibility, 74.6 percent of the electors voted for Fox's enshrinement in the Hall. However, Hall of Fame rules require that a candidate receive at least 75 percent of electors' votes. So when you visit Cooperstown, New York, you won't find a plaque with the name Nellie Fox, despite baseball's long-standing tradition of rounding all fractions upward.* Does Nellie Fox deserve to be in the Hall of Fame? Probably. Is it sad and unfortunate that he was not elected? Definitely.

Or take the great Yankee shortstop Phil Rizzuto. He isn't in the Hall of Fame but everyone knows he should be, especially now that Pee Wee Reese is.

Or take this fugue, F Major Book Two. You won't find F Major Book Two in my Top Ten. But if my Top Ten were a Top Eleven, I would add F Major Book Two without a second thought. This fugue has all the elements: a great subject, a long and wonderful second episode, and a dynamic and clear overall structure.

*For example, Enos Slaughter's lifetime batting average is .2998. But if you look in the *Baseball Encyclopedia,* you will find Slaughter's lifetime batting average listed as .300.

LISTENER'S GUIDE
to the F Major Fugue
WELL–TEMPERED CLAVIER
Book Two

PRELUDE

This prelude has lines moving at various speeds; listen for them.

VOICES

3

MAJOR FEATURE AND SPECIAL DEVICE

The second episode is monster-sized.

FORM

First entry in the soprano; second entry in the alto; codetta (very long); third entry in the bass; first episode (short); fourth entry in the bass; second episode (very, very long); fifth entry in the alto; third episode (medium-sized); sixth entry in the bass; fourth episode (long); seventh entry in the soprano; eighth entry in the bass; coda.

LISTENING HINTS

1. The codetta is very long, longer than the subject of the fugue.

2. The first episode is very short.

3. The second episode is monster-sized. See the essay for more on this episode.

4. The fourth episode is long but not as long as the second.

5. The eighth and last entry of the subject in the bass is a slight variation of the subject.

To its detractors, the subject might seem to have hiccups. But I love the hiccupy sequence that runs twice at the head of the subject. I also love the pauses, the rests between the hiccups. Whenever I hear the first entry of this fugue, and the rests in the subject, I dream of all the music with which Bach is going to fill those rests.

I like the way Bach filled in the rests in the subject in all the entries after the first entry. But whenever I listen to the beginning of this fugue, there are lingering doubts in my mind that there might have been an even more wonderful way for Bach to fill in the rests in the subject, for example as he did in the C Major Organ Fugue. In the final analysis, these lingering doubts kept this fugue out of my Top Ten.

A Monster!

The second episode is 26 measures long. It takes up more than one quarter of the fugue. It's not overstating things to say that the second episode is monster-sized. And it's remarkable not only for its length, but for its lack of sequences. Of the 26 measures, only six involve sequences — one sequence in the middle of the episode that runs twice and starts to run a third time. Contrast those statistics for the second episode of this fugue with the statistics for another long episode, the fifth episode from C-sharp Major Book Two, which is 14 measures long with 10 measures involved in sequences.

Despite its length and lack of sequences, the second episode is still exciting and leads very well into the fifth entry of the subject. Bach keeps the second episode exciting even without using a device such as having one voice rest during the episode and then having the voice that's resting come in with a dramatic entry of the subject after the episode.

This whole fugue inherits a light, happy, and carefree feeling from its subject, but the episodes have a sufficiently different texture from the subject for the entries of the subject to stand out and provide easily recognizable structural landmarks.

f minor

BOOK TWO

QUESTION: WHAT is it that precedes you wherever you go?

Answer: Your reputation.

Often, this reputation is deserved. For example, if the Boston Red Sox were in an important game in the pennant race, or somehow managed to make it to the playoffs or World Series, you could bet that they would lose because they totally deserve their reputation as being the biggest chokers in baseball history (for example, in 1978 against the Yankees, in 1986 against the Mets). But sometimes the reputation may not be deserved.

Musical keys also have reputations, specifically, for the kinds of pieces written in them. For example, D Major is known as "the key of kings" because trumpets and bugles in the time of Bach and before could play only in D Major, so fanfares for kings often had to be written in D Major. Thus D Major got its reputation for being happy, triumphant, in a word majestic. This reputation then extended beyond fanfares into all kinds of music.

F minor, the key of this fugue, has a very different reputation. Pieces written in f minor have the reputation of being slow, emotional, highly chromatic (many added sharps and flats), even languid. A typical example is the f minor fugue Book One, an emotional piece with a very slow first subject and many added chromatics.

Even this fugue's prelude, the f minor prelude Book Two, while not overly chromatic, is slow and very emotional. However, when I listen to the fugue I think: maybe the Red Sox will win the World Series one day.

LISTENER'S GUIDE
to the f minor Fugue
WELL–TEMPERED CLAVIER
Book Two

PRELUDE

Much slower and more emotional than the fugue; should be played on the clavichord?

VOICES

3

MAJOR FEATURES

Excellent subject.

Strong move to the relative major in episode 1, and entries 4 and 5. Four-times-used sequence in the first episode, second episode, fourth episode, and coda. Note that the sequence unit of the sequence always runs twice and starts to run a third time before breaking.

SPECIAL DEVICES

Stretto. This is a fugue that hardly uses stretto at all.

FORM

First entry in the soprano; second entry in the alto; codetta; third entry in the bass; first episode, first time for the sequence, strong move to the relative major; fourth entry in the soprano in major; fifth entry in the alto in major; second episode, second time for the sequence; sixth entry in the bass in minor; third episode, the only episode that doesn't use the sequence; seventh entry in the alto; fourth episode, a triple episode with three sequences (the third sequence of the three sequences in this episode is the third time the repeated sequence runs); eighth entry in the soprano, ninth and last entry in the alto in stretto overlapping the eighth entry by three notes; coda, fourth and last time the repeated sequence runs in this fugue.

As a whole, this fugue is completely different from the reputation of a piece in f minor. It is fast, lively, and doesn't have a lot of added sharps or flats. But it has inherited from f minor a sharp, almost biting quality not present in other minor keys such as a minor, d minor, e minor, or b minor.

This fugue is also a member of the Top Ten. The wonderful, distinct subject, the strong move to the relative major (first episode, entries 4 and 5; see the Listener's Guide), as well as the clear and excellent episodes, especially the four-times-used sequence (episodes 1, 2, 4, and the coda) make this one of the best fugues in the *Well-Tempered*.

As we've seen, this fugue, c minor Book One, E-flat Major Book One, and C Major Book Two so resemble each other that they form a family. Understanding the family relationships will make it more interesting to listen to any one of the four fugues, since we will be listening not only to that fugue but also for its similarities and connections with the other fugues. Also, this family of four helps us to understand the organization of the *Well-Tempered* on a level larger than that of a single fugue.

C Major Book Two and c minor Book One are first cousins. This fugue, f minor Book Two, is a distant relative of both, and E-flat Major is a long-lost relative of the other three.

C minor Book One and C Major Book Two share the following characteristics:

1. The head of the subject of each fugue has exactly the same rhythm.

2. The distinction between episodes and entries is extremely clear in both fugues. They are very easy to follow.

3. Both fugues have three voices.

4. Both fugues have four episodes.

5. The first and fourth episodes of both fugues are sequential and canonic. The fourth episode in both fugues is a double episode whose first sequence is the same as the sequence in the first episode.

6. Both fugues have strange endings. The C Major fugue has no last entry, while the c minor fugue has an extra entry in the coda. (See D Major Book One for more on strange endings.)

7. Both fugues have the same order of entry in their expositions: alto, soprano, bass.

8. Both are simple fugues.

You can see why these two fugues are first cousins.

This fugue, f minor Book Two, is a distant relative of C Major Book Two and c minor Book One, probably on C Major Book Two's side because of the more prevalent use of groups of four sixteenths in f minor Book Two and C Major Book Two than in c minor Book One. Similarities include:

1. The distinction between episodes and entries is very clear.

2. All three use a sequence more than once.

3. All three have three voices.

4. All three are simple fugues.

F minor Book Two is more distantly related to C Major Book Two and c minor Book One than they are to each other because of important differences between f minor Book Two, on the one hand, and c minor Book One and C Major Book Two on the other. Here are some of the differences:

1. The repeated sequence in the f minor fugue is used four times, as opposed to twice in C Major Book Two and c minor Book One.

2. The twice-used sequence in C Major Book Two and c minor Book One is canonic; the four-times-used sequence in the f minor fugue is not.

3. The head of the subject of f minor Book Two does not share the rhythmic similarity of the heads of the subjects of C Major Book Two and c minor Book One.

4. F minor Book Two is not as simple as C Major Book Two and c minor Book One.

Finally, E-flat Major Book One is very distantly related to the other three.

There are some similarities among all four fugues — three voices, use of a repeated sequence, and a much clearer distinction between episodes and entries than in most other fugues in the *Well-Tempered*. The very important differences between the E-flat Major fugue and the other three make its relationship to them very distant. The most important of these is that the boundary and distinction to the listener between episodes and entries, while still present in the E-flat Major, are much less sharp than in the other three.

An Unanswered Question

This is a FUGUE THAT HARDLY USES STRETTO AT ALL. Remember that a fugue that hardly uses stretto at all has at most one pair of stretto entries, and even those two entries only overlap slightly. In this fugue only the second-to-last and last entries, entries 8 and 9 (see the Listener's Guide), are in stretto, and the ninth entry overlaps only the last three notes of the eighth entry.

Since there is so little stretto, why did Bach use any at all? The large number of fugues that hardly use stretto at all in the *Well-Tempered*, four, would seem to indicate that Bach had some reason for using only a tiny amount of stretto in a fugue.

Name That Fugue

In the 1970s there was a TV show called "Name That Tune," featuring two contestants competing in various tune-naming rounds to determine that night's champion. The champion then played one more tune-naming game for additional money.

The most exciting of the tune-naming games was the one in which the two contestants bid for tunes. The host would read a clue, and then one player would announce in how many notes he or she could name the tune, as in, "I can name that tune in six notes." (Seven was the maximum number of notes for the first bid.) The next player would then have to bid a lower number of notes or otherwise challenge the first contestant to "Name That Tune." When challenged, the first player would have to name the tune after hearing only the number of bid notes. This process of bidding continued until the number of notes got down to one, or until one player was challenged to "name that tune."

The reason the bidding portion of the show always held our attention was that the players were able to name tunes based only on a simple clue and precious few notes, tunes that many people in the audience could hardly remember if they heard the whole song sung with its lyrics.

If we played "Name That Fugue" with Bach's fugues, the wonder would be that anyone could tell one fugue from another by only the first few notes of the subject. There are 48 fugues in the *Well-Tempered* and literally hundreds of other fugues by Bach. Yet it is possible to distinguish each of these fugues merely by hearing the beginning of their subjects. And that is possible because Bach designed and wrote the beginning of each of his fugue subjects, the head, to be unique and distinct. This is a testament to Bach's immense creativity.

Another important point about the subjects of Bach's fugues is that if two fugues have similar (not the same) subjects, usually not only the subjects but also the entire fugues are similar. Prime examples are the c minor fugue Book One and the C Major fugue Book Two.

Fingerprints

In "Name That Fugue" we said it was possible to distinguish one fugue from any other fugue by only the first few notes of its subject. More generally, it is possible to distinguish one of Bach's pieces from any other of Bach's pieces by only the first few notes of the pieces' themes. Bach had an unbelievable creative ability to invent wonderful, recognizable, and different themes for all the thousands of pieces and many thousands of movements he wrote.

In "Name That Fugue" we also said that if two fugues have similar subjects, as, for example, c minor Book One and C Major Book Two, then the entire fugues themselves are similar. This is also true for Bach's works in general: if two pieces have similar themes, then they are similar in their entirety.

We call the theme of a piece a FINGERPRINT for the piece. It really isn't a surprise that for Bach the theme was a fingerprint for his pieces. Given his immense creativity, musical memory, and desire not to repeat himself, it makes a lot of sense that Bach invented a recognizable and different theme for each piece and movement.

What does come as a surprise is that there is *another* characteristic of Bach's pieces that serves as a fingerprint. This other characteristic is a piece's cadence structure. To understand what that is, we have to understand what a cadence is.

A CADENCE is simply the music that marks the end of a piece or a pause within a piece. Though the technical musical description of a cadence can get pretty complicated, it is very easy to hear a cadence bring a piece or a section of a piece to a conclusion.

The word comes from the Latin verb *cado,* meaning to fall. Cadence got its name because originally during it the highest part would "fall" by three, four, five, or more steps. This practice of having the highest part fall downward during the cadence has continued, though to a much lesser extent, through Bach's time and on into the present.

Now, you might recognize that a cadence alone could not be a fingerprint because there are just a limited number of possible chord combinations to use in a cadence (though Bach utilized far more combinations than anyone else). There just aren't enough possible cadences to go around for all the thousands of Bach's pieces and movements within pieces.

That's where the CADENCE STRUCTURE comes in. By this I mean not only the cadence itself but also the number of cadences or pauses within a piece; the strength of the pauses (that is, full stops, half stops); and where the cadences come. Considering that many of Bach's pieces are 50 or 100 or 200 measures long, just in terms of various placements for cadences, let alone all the possibilities for various numbers and strengths of cadences, there are more than enough cadence structures to go around for all Bach's pieces and movements.

So cadence structure is another fingerprint for Bach's pieces. No two pieces have the same cadence structure, and if two pieces have similar cadence structures, as, for example, do many of the *Goldberg Variations,* then the pieces are similar in their entirety. In addition, within any particular piece by Bach the actual cadences, the chords themselves used at the end of the piece or at a pause in the piece, are virtually identical throughout the piece. We call the cadences themselves the ACTUAL CADENCES to distinguish them from the cadence structure of the piece.

Actually, it shouldn't come as a great surprise that the cadence structure is a fingerprint for Bach's pieces. Because one of the most important parts of the details of a piece is its cadence structure, it is no wonder that Bach invented a different cadence structure for each of his pieces and movements of pieces.

An interesting question is whether there are fingerprints for Bach's pieces other than the theme and the cadence structure. If you find one, please let me know.

F–sharp Major
BOOK TWO

WE ALL know the story "The Boy Who Cried Wolf." The lesson of it is that if you cry for help when you don't need it, then people won't believe you when you really do and won't help you. The analogy for composers is: don't use the same device or phrase too often in a piece. Otherwise, when you want to use the device in an important way, the audience will not respond, having become accustomed and indifferent to it.

In this fugue Bach reveals a profound understanding of the lesson of the "Boy Who Cried Wolf." The subject contains two pairs of sixteenth notes. Bach could have used sixteenth notes throughout the fugue, especially pairs of sixteenth notes, while still keeping the fugue motivic. However, had he done so, the sixteenth notes in the subject would not be effective because they would not stand out much from sixteenth notes in the rest of the fugue.

Instead, in this 84-measure fugue, Bach uses only three pairs of sixteenth notes other than the sixteenth notes in the entries of the subject. Slow eighth notes and quarter notes predominate. So the sixteenth notes in the subject and thus the whole subject stand out. The subject, by the way, begins with a long trill.

Canonic Sequence

This fugue has a great canonic sequence, which Bach uses in the second and fourth episodes and also in the coda. The canon is

LISTENER'S GUIDE
to the F-sharp Major Fugue
WELL-TEMPERED CLAVIER
Book Two

PRELUDE

A member of my Top Ten Preludes.

VOICES

3

MAJOR FEATURE

A trill in the subject.

SPECIAL DEVICE

Episodes 2 and 4 are sequential and canonic.

FORM

First entry in the alto; second entry in the soprano; third entry in the bass; first episode; fourth entry in the soprano; second episode; fifth entry in the bass; sixth entry in the alto; seventh entry in the soprano in minor; third episode; eighth entry in the alto in minor; fourth episode; ninth entry in the bass in major; two measures; tenth entry in the alto; two measures; eleventh and last entry in the soprano; coda.

---

between the soprano and the alto with the bass free from the canon. The voices taking part in the canon use quarter notes taken from the end of the subject, and the bass uses eighth notes very similar to the eighth notes from the subject.

Preludes II

One of the great joys of being a fan is arguing. There is no greater pleasure than to walk away from an argument about a player or a team or a piece or a song knowing that you have convinced the other person that you are right, even if the other person won't admit it. (If someone actually *admits* that you are right, then that person wasn't worth arguing with.) Besides its sheer entertainment value, arguing is helpful since it forces us to decide exactly which pieces are our favorites, allows us to extol these favorite pieces, and forces us to consider and expound upon our reasons for loving them. In *The Essential Listener's Guide* I established the Top Ten as a forum for argument.

The purpose of this box is to facilitate arguments about the preludes. Below are listed expertly selected preludes and perfectly selected instrumentations for those preludes. Go ahead and argue with my selection of preludes and my instrumentations. Please!

SELECTED PRELUDES FROM THE *WELL-TEMPERED* AND INSTRUMENTATIONS FOR THEM

PIECE	INSTRUMENTATION
Book One	
C Major	brass quintet
c minor	two kazoos
	or
	oboe and bassoon
	or
	violin and cello
C-sharp Major	flute and cello
	or
	violin and cello
D Major	trumpet and two trombones
d minor	violin and cello
E-flat Major	string quartet
E Major	flute, clarinet, and bassoon
F Major	string quartet
F-sharp Major	any pair of a soprano and a bass instrument
f-sharp minor	two guitars
	or
	flute and guitar
	or
	violin and cello
G Major	two players who can play like the wind
g minor	piano, violin, cello
A-flat Major	two guitars and one violin
g-sharp minor	two violins, cello
B Major	piano, violin, cello
Book Two	
C Major	brass quintet and tympani
	or
	steel drums and maracas
c minor	violin and cello
C-sharp Major	string quartet
d minor	violin and cello
F-sharp Major	viola and cello
f-sharp minor	flute, clarinet, bassoon
G Major	flute, solo violin, strings, and harpsichord (just like Brandenburg Concerto No. 5)

A-flat Major	violin and cello
a minor	two xylophones or two metallophones
B Major	recorder and bassoon
b minor	violin and cello

Notes:

1. A heartfelt performance is much more important than any particular instrumentation.

2. All the instrumentations listed above should not present undue difficulties to perform, except possibly that for A-flat Major Book Two.

3. A remarkable number of the preludes from the *Well-Tempered* are duets — approximately 12 from Book One and nine from Book Two.

f–sharp minor
BOOK TWO

WHEN DISCUSSING double fugues I said that, just as too many cooks can spoil the broth, too many subjects can spoil a fugue. For TRIPLE FUGUES — fugues with three subjects — the danger of utter confusion for the audience is worse. Let me give two examples.

In a double fugue there are four possible arrangements for running the subjects — run the first subject alone, run the second subject alone, run both subjects at the same time, or run no subject at all. In a triple fugue there are eight possibilities — run the first subject alone, the second subject alone, the third subject alone, the first and second subject, the first and third subject, the second and third subject, all three subjects together, or no subjects at all. A triple fugue is more than twice as complicated as a double fugue.

In a double fugue, the two subjects can be exposed separately and then combine later, or they can be exposed together. I can't even calculate how many possible ways there are to expose the subjects in a triple fugue! But the situation isn't completely hopeless. A successful triple fugue is possible if the composer uses the most extreme care to avoid a swift descent into the abyss of audience confusion.

Typically, the planning of a fugue begins with the subject. For triple fugues the construction of the subjects is critical. Poor subjects, either alone or in combination, will lead straight to disaster. But good subjects alone are not enough. Even the most perfect three subjects, if not used in a clear overall structure, will lead to confusion.

LISTENER'S GUIDE
to the f-sharp minor Fugue
WELL-TEMPERED CLAVIER
Book Two

PRELUDE

Nice moving soprano line and move to major.

VOICES

3

MAJOR FEATURE AND SPECIAL DEVICE

A triple fugue. Since there are only two places in the fugue where Bach runs entries of two or more subjects at the same time, it shouldn't be too hard to follow all entries of each subject.

FORM

First entry of the first subject in the alto; second entry of the first subject in the soprano; codetta; third entry of the first subject in the bass; first episode; fourth entry of the first subject in the soprano; two measures; first entry of the second subject in the bass; second entry of the second subject in the alto; third entry of the second subject in the soprano; fourth entry of the second subject in the alto; fifth entry of the second subject in the alto; sixth entry of the second subject in the soprano; seventh entry of the second subject in the bass; one measure; eighth entry of the second subject in the alto; ninth entry of the second subject in the soprano; tenth entry of the second subject in the bass; eleventh entry of the second subject in the soprano; twelfth entry of the second subject in the alto; fifth entry of the first subject in the alto, thirteenth entry of the second subject in the soprano, fourteenth entry of the second subject in the bass; one measure; fifteenth entry of the second subject in the soprano; sixth entry of the first subject in the bass, sixteenth entry of the second subject in the soprano, seventeenth entry of the second subject in the alto; first entry of the third subject in the alto; second entry of the third subject in the soprano; third entry of the third subject in the bass; fourth entry of the third subject in the alto; fifth entry of the third subject in the bass; sixth entry of the third subject in the alto; one measure; seventh entry of the third subject in the bass; eighth entry of the third subject in the soprano; one measure; ninth entry of the third subject in the soprano; second episode; seventh entry of the first subject in the alto; first time for all three subjects together: eighth entry of the first subject in the soprano, tenth entry of the third subject in the bass, eighteenth entry of the second subject in the alto; third episode; second time for all three subjects together: ninth entry of the first subject in the bass, eleventh entry of the third subject in the soprano, nineteenth entry of the second subject in the alto; fourth episode; tenth entry of the first subject in the soprano, twelfth entry of the third subject in the alto, twentieth entry of the second subject in the bass; coda.

LISTENING HINTS

1. This fugue looks complicated, but it isn't so bad!

2. The second subject is very short.

3. For the end of the fugue, I recommend sitting back and hearing that all three subjects are combining, rather than listening for specific entries of the subjects.

Bach has constructed the wonderful f-sharp minor Book Two by using three wonderful subjects and an overall structure that is clear and very easy to follow.

The first subject has more than one idea, while the second and third subjects are monothematic but different from each other. The first subject is moderately long, nearly three measures, and very interesting and exciting. It contains many different melodic and rhythmic ideas — steps and jumps; eighth notes, sixteenth notes, quarter notes tied to eighth notes, and a half note.

While the first subject is fairly long and contains many different ideas, the second subject is short and monothematic, just a four-note downward-moving scale.

The long/short difference between the first and second subjects leads to additional variety. Because of this fugue's length there is a fairly substantial time interval between entries of the first subject. But because the second subject is so short, Bach is able to run many entries of it in rapid succession. Bach uses 17 entries of the second subject in a 15-measure stretch (without stretto), compared with only 10 entries of the first subject in the entire 70-measure fugue.

Despite being monothematic, the second subject does contain a lively touch of rhythmic variety: it consists, in order, of an eighth note, a dotted eighth note, a sixteenth note, and another eighth note. The dotted-eighth note/sixteenth-note combination is the second subject's distinguishing feature.

After an introductory eighth note, the third subject contains only sixteenth notes. The third subject consists of a sequence — two groups of four sixteenth notes — repeated twice. Besides its obvious rhythmic differences from the other two subjects, the third subject with its repeating pattern provides great contrast to the completely unpatterned second subject, and the first subject that has only a hint of a repeated pattern. The third subject is also intermediate in length between the long first subject and the short second subject.

For this fugue Bach has used a very simple but effective overall structure: as much as possible, he avoids running more than one subject at the same time, and combines all three subjects only near the end of the fugue and in an easily heard manner.

G Major

BOOK TWO

THIS FUGUE, G Major Book Two, is one of two fugues from the *Well-Tempered* for which there exists an earlier version. (A-flat Major Book Two is the other.) Bach made three major changes to the original version of this fugue.

The first major change was structural: he more than doubled the length of the second episode, from 8 measures to 20 measures.

The second major change was more subtle. Through the first half of the fugue up until the fifth entry, Bach kept the bass part the same as in the original version but changed harmonies in the upper two parts above the bass line.

Bach had a lot of experience harmonizing the same line in different ways, having harmonized hundreds and probably thousands of chorales earlier in his life. (CHORALE, recall, is the word for a hymn sung in a Lutheran church service.) Many of the melodies for the chorales are folk tunes. Other melodies were written specifically for the Lutheran service, some by Martin Luther himself. The melodies for the chorales were known by the congregation, and it was the job of the church organist or choir director to write harmonies for them.

More than 350 chorale harmonizations by J. S. Bach exist; undoubtedly there are hundreds that have been lost, and hundreds more that Bach improvised during a service and never wrote down. Among existing Bach chorales, we have some that he harmonized in two different ways, and some in three different ways. There are chorales that Bach harmonized in four and five different ways, and

LISTENER'S GUIDE
to the G Major Fugue
WELL-TEMPERED CLAVIER
Book Two

there is even one that he harmonized in *six* different ways. Bach's experience with harmonization and reharmonization served him well when it came time to reharmonize the upper two parts in the first half of this fugue.

This piece holds the title for the fugue in the *Well-Tempered* with the fewest entries of the subject: it has only six. All other fugues in the *Well-Tempered* have at least eight, and the average number of entries is 12. Bach generally uses many entries of the subject in his fugues because the subject is the star of a fugue, and Bach wants to highlight the star. One factor in this fugue's small number of entries is the length of its subject: at six measures, it is one of the longest subjects in the *Well-Tempered*. The six entries of the subject of this fugue manage to occupy half of this 72-measure fugue, right around the average percentage occupancy of a fugue in the *Well-Tempered* by entries of its subject.

The third major alteration Bach made to the original version of this fugue concerns its ending. In the original version the end seems abrupt, coming right after the sixth and last entry that follows the short second episode. In the final version, Bach lengthened the second episode and also added some fast scales before the sixth entry to help the fugue come to a smoother end. But even the new ending, with the fast scales, sounds a little out of place. It's strange that Bach seemed to have trouble trying to figure out how to end this fugue. Usually, Bach is the master of endings.

Listener's Guide to BWV 902

G Major Book Two is one of two fugues from the *Well-Tempered* for which there exists an earlier version. The three major changes Bach made in the second version are:

1. He lengthened the second episode from eight measures in the original to 20 measures in the final version, adding a sequence or two along the way.

2. The last entry in the original version is in the bass, while the last entry in the final version is in the alto.

3. In the beginning of the fugue (up until the start of the fifth entry) Bach kept the bass exactly the same from the original to the final version, but changed the upper parts.

In the original version, also a three-voice fugue, Bach even adds an extra voice in the middle section, specifically during the first episode and fourth entry. The extra voice helps make for full chords that accompany the one part with fast-moving notes. It is rare for Bach to add extra voices to a fugue except at the end of a piece, and the chords accompanying the moving line may well just have been left as markers of the harmony by Bach to be filled in at some later date. In the final version the extra voice is gone, and the chords have often been replaced by additional moving lines.

Note that the ends of both the original and final versions are somewhat unique and strange. The end of the original version seems to be a bit abrupt, while the end to the final version features the unusual appearance of some very fast scales. Bach may have been unsure exactly how to end this fugue.

Bach was also very ambivalent about the prelude for this fugue. For the original version of the fugue Bach wrote not one but two different preludes, one very long and one very short. For the fugue in Book Two of the *Well-Tempered,* Bach wrote a *third* prelude whose length is between the very long and the very short preludes. Here is the Listener's Guide to BWV 902. The fugue is known as a FUGHETTA, or "little fugue."

LISTENER'S GUIDE
to the Prelude and Fughetta in G Major (BWV 902)
Original Version of the G Major Fugue
WELL–TEMPERED CLAVIER
Book Two

PRELUDE

Bach wrote two preludes for this fugue. One is very short and is listed with this fugue as BWV 902. The other prelude is very long and is listed separately as BWV 902a.

VOICES

3

MAJOR FEATURES

A quick, lively subject.
A somewhat abrupt ending.

SPECIAL DEVICE

An extra voice during the first episode and fourth and sixth entries.

FORM

First entry in the soprano; second entry in the alto; third entry in the bass; first episode; fourth entry in the bass in minor; fifth entry in the soprano in minor; second episode; sixth and last entry in the bass; coda.

LISTENING HINTS

1. The first episode is pretty long.
2. The fifth entry in the soprano comes in immediately after the fourth entry in the bass.
3. Bach adds an extra voice during the first episode and fourth and sixth entries.

g minor

BOOK TWO

IT IS uncommon for Bach to repeat a note in the melody of a piece even twice, rare for him to repeat a note in the melody four times, and singular for him to repeat a note more than four times. As can easily be heard, the subject of this fugue contains a note that is repeated *seven* times.

Another distinctive feature of this fugue is the simultaneous entries of the subject: entries 9 and 10, 11 and 12, and 13 and 14 run at the same time. They are STRETTO ENTRIES THAT OVERLAP COMPLETELY. The subject of this fugue — with all its rests, predominant use of slow notes, and lack of twists and turns in the melody — is particularly well suited for completely overlapping entries. If the subject had too many fast notes or a melody that was too intricate, completely overlapping entries would sound like a knotty, confusing mess.

Three other fugues in the *Well-Tempered* (b-flat minor Book One, d-sharp minor Book Two, and b-flat minor Book Two) use completely overlapping entries. Two of those, b-flat minor Book One and d-sharp minor Book Two, use only one pair of completely overlapping entries.

The third easily heard feature of this fugue is the ultraconsistent countersubject. The countersubject, which makes interesting use of sixteenth notes, eighth notes, and sixteenth-note rests, runs against all the entries of the subject (except for the first entry). When entries of the subject run simultaneously (completely overlapping entries) in two voices, the countersubject still runs in a third voice. There is

LISTENER'S GUIDE
to the g minor Fugue
WELL-TEMPERED CLAVIER
Book Two

PRELUDE

Bach marked this prelude *largo* to indicate that it should be played very, very slowly.

VOICES

4

MAJOR FEATURE

One note in the subject is repeated seven times.

SPECIAL DEVICES

Completely overlapping entries. Three pairs of entries (entries 9–10, 11–12, and 13–14) overlap completely.

Consistent countersubject. The countersubject in this fugue accompanies all the entries of the subject except the first.

FORM

First entry in the tenor; second entry in the alto; third entry in the soprano; fourth entry in the bass; first episode; fifth entry in the tenor; second episode; sixth entry in the alto; seventh entry in the soprano in major; eighth entry in the bass in major; third episode; ninth and tenth entries simultaneously in the alto and tenor in minor; fourth episode; eleventh and twelfth entries simultaneously in the soprano and alto; fifth episode; thirteenth and fourteenth entries simultaneously in the tenor and bass; sixth episode, fake entry in the tenor; fifteenth entry in the soprano; seventh episode; sixteenth and last entry in the bass; coda.

LISTENING HINTS

1. The last entry is a slightly modified version of the subject.

2. The fourth, fifth, and seventh episodes are very short.

even one occasion (entries 13 and 14) when the subject runs in two voices and the countersubject in the other two voices.

As is usual in Bach's fugues, this countersubject is counter to, or different from, the subject in terms of rhythm and amount of motion. While the subject uses mainly slow notes, rests, and repeated notes, the countersubject mostly employs fast notes that move up and down. The fast-moving notes in the countersubject are especially noticeable during the seven-times-repeated note in the subject.

My award for the best countersubject in the *Well-Tempered* goes to this fugue's countersubject. It is fine music in its own right. It also does such an excellent job of complementing the subject that you almost forget it is there.

A–flat Major

BOOK TWO

WHERE I went to camp there used to be a game called "tooling" (sounds like fooling). There are many forms of tooling, but the most popular was the "name tool." The person performing the name tool would stand near a tree or building and shout out a common name such as Jon, David, or Barbara, duck behind the building or tree, and then watch as three or four people named Jon, David, or Barbara turned around to see who had called them. Not wanting to be tooled, you quickly learned not to turn around when you heard your name. After I returned home from camp, it used to take me a few weeks to begin to respond again when someone would call my name. In this fugue, A flat Major Book Two, it seems that Bach may be playing a tool of his own.

The first entry of the subject is in the alto. The second entry is in the soprano. Following the second entry of the subject, Bach uses a FAKE ENTRY of the subject in the alto. Specifically, the alto runs the first half of the subject, making you think that you are about to hear an entry of the entire subject. Listen to the fugue. You'll be faked.

Why did Bach use a fake entry? Why did he use it in the exposition, where a fake entry of the subject can confuse the audience about the number of voices in the fugue, and thus possibly confuse them for the remainder of the fugue? My initial explanation, and the initial explanation of everyone I talked to, was that the fake entry was some kind of joke or tool that Bach was playing on the audience.

The trouble with the tool explanation is that Bach was not one for capricious jokes in a serious piece such as a fugue from the

LISTENER'S GUIDE
to the A-flat Major Fugue
WELL–TEMPERED CLAVIER
Book Two

PRELUDE

Despite having no repeated sections, this prelude is one of the longest in the *Well-Tempered.*

VOICES

4

MAJOR FEATURE

There is a fake entry of the subject between the second and third entries.

SPECIAL DEVICE

This is a fugue that hardly uses stretto at all. Entries 13 and 14 overlap slightly.

FORM

First entry in the alto; second entry in the soprano; fake entry in the alto; third entry in the tenor; fourth entry in the bass; first episode; fifth entry in the bass; one measure; sixth entry in the soprano; seventh entry in the alto; second episode; eighth entry in the soprano; ninth entry in the alto; third episode, move to minor; tenth entry in the tenor in minor; one measure; eleventh entry in the soprano in minor; twelfth entry in the bass in major; fourth episode; thirteenth entry in the tenor, fourteenth entry in the bass in stretto; fifth episode, fermata, more fifth episode; fifteenth entry in the tenor.

LISTENING HINTS

1. Beware the fake entry between the second and third entries. See the essay for more on the fake entry.

2. The first episode is unusually long.

Well-Tempered. Even though I didn't think the tool explanation was a good one, for a long time I couldn't think of a better one, and neither could anyone I talked to. But now I am pretty certain that I know why Bach used a fake entry of the subject in the exposition of this fugue, and we can all thank a friend of mine named Jim for the following brilliant explanation.

People on airplanes generally don't like wearing seatbelts. When the seatbelt sign goes off, people loosen their seatbelts, take them off, and sometimes even walk around in the aisles. When the plane goes through turbulence, they all rush back to their seats, put their seatbelts on, and tighten them. People do this because the turbulence signals danger. Fortunately, almost always nothing further happens, but something *could* happen, and the turbulence is a warning.

In the same way, the fake entry in the exposition of this fugue is a warning that anything might happen. If Bach is willing to take the dangerous and potentially very confusing step of using a fake entry of the subject, then he could conceivably do anything. Just as the plane probably will not crash, Bach probably will not use too many surprising compositional moves. But he might, and the fake entry alerts us to what he could do. The fake entry is a warning to us to listen to the fugue with open ears.

Two Versions

This 50-measure fugue is one of two in the *Well-Tempered* — G Major Book Two is the other — for which there exists an earlier version, consisting of the first 24 measures of this fugue. The original version was written in F Major, not in A-flat Major. Now Bach might have needed a fugue in A-flat Major for Book Two, so he TRANSPOSED (changed the key of) the original version from F Major to A-flat Major. But the 24-measure version of this fugue takes only about one and a half minutes to perform, and thus this fugue would have been one of the shortest in the *Well Tempered*. Bach may have felt that the fugue needed to be lengthened.

How did he lengthen it? The original version concludes with the eighth entry of the subject in the soprano. Notice that all of the first eight entries are in major. In the additional 26 measures of this fugue, Bach takes his time making a strong move to minor. From the very beginning of the additional material — entry 9 in the alto — Bach is foreshadowing a move to minor. The move to minor appears in full blossom with the tenth and eleventh entries.

In this longer version of the fugue Bach uses a grand ending, compared with the very simple ending of the original version. At the end Bach first has an entry of the subject in the bass (entry 14), and then the bass plays fast notes while the other three voices play chords in unison. Bach then has a complete pause, or FERMATA, before continuing on with the fifth episode. Bach even adds an extra voice during the last entry.

Should Bach Have Quit
While He Was Ahead?

As I mentioned, A-flat Major Book Two is one of two fugues from the *Well-Tempered* for which there exists an earlier version. G Major Book Two is the other. While for G Major Book Two Bach made alterations in the original version by lengthening one episode, adding an entry, and making some changes in the soprano and alto parts, for A-flat Major Book Two Bach did not touch the original version but merely doubled its length, adding 26 measures to the original, intact 24 measures.

Also, Bach changed the key of the original, F Major, to A-flat Major for the final version, to get a fugue in A-flat Major for Book Two of the *Well-Tempered*. This is not the only case where Bach transposed a piece from one key to another to fill out the *Well-Tempered*. The C-sharp Major fugue Book One, for example, was originally written in C Major. I happen to think this fugue sounds much better in F Major. A-flat Major is just a wimpy key in a well-tempered scale.

The original version of the A-flat Major fugue Book Two and its prelude (different from the prelude in the *Well-Tempered*) are catalogued as BWV 901. There is no reason to give a Listener's Guide to BWV 901 since it is exactly the same as that for the A-flat Major fugue Book Two, concluding with the eighth entry in the soprano.

Should Bach have quit after the original 24 measures, or was he right to continue and add 26 more measures? On the one hand, I love the compact original: four-voice exposition, long episode, then three more entries, one more short episode, and the final entry in the soprano. On the other hand, I like the move to minor and then back to major in the latter 26 measures of the long version of the fugue. On the first hand . . .

g-sharp minor
BOOK TWO

A LONG, moderately slow, minor subject. A monothematic subject that jumps and wanders up and down. A fugue 143 measures long, longer than any other fugue in the *Well-Tempered*.

Sounds like this fugue, g-sharp minor Book Two, is a strong candidate for my Long, Slow, and Not My Favorite Club. Not so, not even close, because of a very interesting second subject, which enters two measures after the end of the seventh entry of the first subject in the bass.

The second subject first descends and then ascends chromatically by step. To borrow a phrase from Mr. Spock, first officer of the *U.S.S. Enterprise*, it sounds fascinating. Bach used similar fascinating chromatic lines in a number of pieces he wrote late in life — for example, the third subject of the eleventh fugue from the *Art of the Fugue*.

G-sharp minor Book Two is a curious cross between the two types of double fugues we have discussed, and demonstrates another of the numerous possible combinations and permutations for double fugues. In this fugue, the second subject is exposed separately beginning after the end of the seventh entry of the first subject. After four autonomous entries, the second subject loses its independence, and for the rest of the fugue accompanies all other entries of the first subject. Notice how beginning with its exposition, the chromatic motive of the second subject permeates the piece.

While this fugue has a unique structure as a double fugue, in one way it is similar to most of the other fugues in the *Well-Tempered*,

LISTENER'S GUIDE
to the g-sharp minor Fugue
WELL–TEMPERED CLAVIER
Book Two

PRELUDE

Almost a member of my Top Ten Preludes. This prelude has a nice move to major, and it reminds me of the preludes in c minor Book One and d minor Book Two.

VOICES

3

MAJOR FEATURES

Double fugue with an intriguing second subject.

At 143 measures, the longest fugue in the *Well-Tempered*.

SPECIAL DEVICES

Double fugue.

FORM

First entry of the first subject in the soprano; second entry of the first subject in the alto; codetta; third entry of the first subject in the bass; first episode, (very short); fourth entry of the first subject in the alto; second episode; fifth entry of the first subject in the bass; third episode; sixth entry of the first subject in the soprano; fourth episode; seventh entry of the first subject in the bass; two measures; first entry of the second subject in the soprano; second entry of the second subject in the alto; third entry of the second subject in the bass; three measures; fourth entry of the second subject in the soprano; fifth episode; eighth entry of the first subject in the bass, fifth entry of the second subject in the alto; two measures; ninth entry of the first subject in the soprano, sixth entry of the second subject in the alto; sixth episode; tenth entry of the first subject in the alto in major, seventh entry of the second subject in the soprano; seventh episode; eleventh entry of the first subject in the alto, eighth entry of the second subject in the bass; eighth episode; twelfth entry of the first subject in the soprano, ninth entry of the second subject in the alto; coda.

LISTENING HINT

The second subject enters two measures after the end of the seventh entry of the first subject in the bass. The second subject initially has four entries independent of the first subject, but then just accompanies all the rest of the entries of the first subject.

single, double, or triple: it has at least two motivic or thematic ideas. Thirty-four of the 38 single fugues in the *Well-Tempered* contain at least two motivic ideas. In double and triple fugues Bach often used MONOTHEMATIC SUBJECTS with only one motivic idea. However, Bach could still provide double and triple fugues with more than one motivic idea by using two or more monothematic subjects with vastly different themes.

Consider the contrasting monothematic subjects in this fugue: The first subject contains only eighth notes, uses a lot of jumps, and has no chromatic notes. The second subject, on the other hand, uses a mixture of eighth notes and quarter notes, moves only by step, and uses a lot of chromatic notes. The two subjects in this fugue complement each other beautifully.

So this fugue is rescued from the Long, Slow, and Not My Favorite Club, and made extremely interesting, by a fascinating second subject.

Monothematic Subjects

Listed here are the fugues from the *Well-Tempered* whose subjects are MONO-THEMATIC — containing only one melodic or rhythmic idea. Listed in italics are those fugues that are not double or triple fugues.

MONOTHEMATIC SUBJECTS IN THE *WELL-TEMPERED*

BOOK ONE	BOOK TWO
c-sharp minor (first subject)	*C-sharp Major*
c-sharp minor (second subject)	c-sharp minor (second subject)
d-sharp minor	*E Major*
f minor (first subject)	f-sharp minor (second subject)
f minor (second subject)	f-sharp minor (third subject)
F-sharp Major (second subject)	g-sharp minor (first subject)
f-sharp minor (first subject)	g-sharp minor (second subject)
f-sharp minor (second subject)	B Major (first subject)
A-flat Major	B Major (second subject)
A Major (first subject)	
A Major (second subject)	

Notice that there are only four fugues in the *Well-Tempered* that have monothematic subjects and that aren't double or triple fugues. Of those four fugues, three — d-sharp minor Book One, C-sharp Major Book Two, and E Major Book Two — have stretto to help balance the monothematicity of the subject. A-flat Major Book One is the only fugue in the *Well-Tempered* that has a monothematic subject, is neither a double nor triple fugue, and has no stretto.

Single fugues need subjects with more than one idea in them, so that the fugue as a whole has more than one motivic idea. In a double fugue or triple fugue, the mono-thematicity of an individual subject can be balanced by a second or a third subject, also monothematic but containing an entirely different idea.

A Major

BOOK TWO

BOTH THE subject and the structure of this fugue are very straight-forward: seventeen of the nineteen notes in the subject are sixteenth notes, most of which move by step. This fugue has no large-level special devices such as stretto or counterexpositions, nor is it a double or triple fugue. But the fugue is not completely uniform. Here we will look at a few of the subtle ways Bach structured the fugue so that the audience would not get bored and not want to listen to it.

The ninth and eleventh notes of the subject are the two notes that are longer than sixteenths. These two notes also fall on beats that usually aren't emphasized. So in each entry of the subject, the two long notes come as a bit of a surprise. The subject is running during 15 of the 29 measures in this fugue. So we spend about half of the fugue being surprised by the long notes in the subject, enough to help keep it interesting and not so much as to ruin the novelty of those long notes. Also, Bach doesn't use the long-note figure anywhere else in the fugue, thus keeping it fresh for the subject.

Bach uses canonic sequences and melodic inversion in the episodes to add further spice to this fugue. The first, third, and fourth episodes have similar canonic sequences. The canon in the first and second episodes is between the soprano and the alto; the canon in the fourth episode is between the alto and the bass. For each of these episodes the material for the sequence unit is taken from the fast notes at the beginning of the subject. The canon in the fourth episode is a CANON IN INVERSION. That is, the alto and the bass run in lines that are the melodic inversion of each other.

LISTENER'S GUIDE
to the A Major Fugue
WELL-TEMPERED CLAVIER
Book Two

PRELUDE

I like following the various moving lines in this prelude.

VOICES

3

MAJOR FEATURE

A subject that keeps driving forward.

SPECIAL DEVICES

Canonic sequences.
Melodic inversion in the episodes.

FORM

First entry in the bass; second entry in the alto; codetta; third entry in the soprano; half a measure; fourth entry in the bass; one measure; fifth entry in the soprano in minor; one measure; sixth entry in the alto in minor; first episode; seventh entry in the bass in major; second episode; eighth entry in the soprano; third episode; ninth entry in the alto; fourth episode; tenth entry in the soprano; coda.

a minor

BOOK TWO

HAVE YOU noticed how the networks have been covering dramatic touchdowns scored in the NFL or Division I-A college football? First they show you a close-up of the celebration in the end zone by the guy who scored. Next they show you a shot of the crowd going crazy. Then comes a picture of the defensive man who got beaten for the touchdown. Next they show the jubilant sideline of the team that scored spilling onto the field. Finally they show you the extra point. All the while, the announcers (very uncharacteristically) remain completely silent and don't say a word.

My guess is that touchdowns are covered like this because the producers and the directors feel that if they showed more than one thing at a time or did not focus on one specific thing, the audience would get confused, and some of the drama of the touchdown would be lost. Even comments by the announcers along with the pictures could distract from the excitement of the moment. Replays, no matter how spectacular the scoring play, are also forbidden, as they, too, are possible unnecessary distractions for the viewers.

In the same vein, a vitally important question for artists is whether or not the audience can hear more than one theme at a time. This fugue, a minor Book Two, answers that question, showing that it is definitely possible for the audience to hear two radically different themes at once.

This is a double fugue, the type in which the two subjects are exposed and developed together. The first subject moves very slowly, while the second subject moves very fast. The first subject moves

LISTENER'S GUIDE
to the a minor Fugue
WELL-TEMPERED CLAVIER
Book Two

PRELUDE
Like the fugue, this prelude uses a lot of chromatic notes and fast-moving rhythms.

VOICES
3

MAJOR FEATURE
A double fugue in which the two subjects are exposed together.

SPECIAL DEVICES
Double fugue.
Sequence used four times (codetta, first episode, third episode, and fifth episode).

FORM
First entry of the first subject in the bass; second entry of the first subject in the alto, second subject in the bass; codetta; third entry of the first subject in the soprano, second subject in the alto; first episode; fourth entry of the first subject in the bass, second subject in the soprano; second episode; fifth entry of the first subject in the soprano, second subject in the alto; third episode; sixth entry of the first subject in the alto, second subject in the bass; fourth episode; seventh entry of the first subject in the soprano, second subject (slightly modified) in the bass; fifth and last episode; eighth and last entry of the first subject in the bass, second subject (really modified) in the soprano; coda.

LISTENING HINT
It may be easier to listen for the second than for the first subject.

only by jumps, while the second subject, except for one jump, moves only by steps.

These important contrasts create a fugue in which the audience is able to hear two different subjects at the same time. In this and in other double fugues of the same type, such as f minor Book One, Bach demonstrates that the audience can follow more than one theme at a time if the artist is careful to make the two themes extremely distinct.

Bach also makes this fugue easier to follow, and therefore compensates for the possible confusion of two subjects running at the same time, by making the structure of the episodes relatively simple: he uses the same sequence in the codetta, the first episode, the third episode, and the end of the fifth episode. The first episode makes my Top Ten Episodes.

B-flat Major
BOOK TWO

A TIME SIGNATURE, as we know, is a symbol composers use at the beginning of a piece to indicate the number of beats in each measure. For example, Bach marked this fugue, B-flat Major Book Two, $\frac{3}{4}$, indicating that each measure contains 3 quarter notes.

In "About Time" we learned about the concept of STRONG and WEAK BEATS in a measure. For each time signature, certain beats in the measure receive more accent and emphasis than other beats. In $\frac{3}{4}$ the strong beats are beats one and three, and beat two is a weak beat. In addition, in $\frac{3}{4}$ the second half of beats one and three are also weakly accented. (The first half of beats one and three receives the strong accent.)

In this fugue Bach departs from the usual practice and gives strong emphasis and accent to the usually weak beats: the subject of this fugue begins on the second half of the first beat of a measure. Many of the harmonies in this fugue also change, and arrive on, the second beat of a measure.

Notice also the pairs of repeated notes in the subject. Typically, when a note is repeated, the repeat receives much less accent than the first time the note is played, and the second note becomes a sort of echo of the first note. However, as you listen to this fugue, you can hear that it is the *second* of the pairs of two notes, the repeat, that receives the accent.

In musical language, the accenting of beats that are usually weak and the accenting of the second, not the first, of a pair of repeated notes, is known as SYNCOPATION.

LISTENER'S GUIDE
to the B-flat Major Fugue
WELL–TEMPERED CLAVIER
Book Two

PRELUDE

One of the longest preludes in the *Well-Tempered.*

VOICES

3

MAJOR FEATURES AND SPECIAL DEVICES

Repeated notes in the subject. Syncopation.

FORM

First entry in the alto; second entry in the soprano; codetta; third entry in the bass; first episode; fourth entry in the bass; second episode; fifth entry in the alto; third episode; sixth entry in the soprano; fourth episode; seventh entry in the bass in minor; fifth episode; eighth entry in the alto in major; sixth episode; ninth entry in the soprano in minor; two measures; tenth entry in the bass in major; seventh episode; eleventh entry in the soprano; coda.

LISTENING HINTS

1. The second episode is long and contains many fake entries and pieces of the subject.

2. All the episodes other than the second are very short.

3. The coda contains many pieces of the subject in different voices.

The syncopation used in this fugue is more subtle than most. Often, syncopation is used in the following more patent and explicit form: while one voice is playing along accenting the usual strong beats, another more prominent voice strongly accents the weak beats. The syncopation used here by Bach — the subject beginning on the weak part of a beat, harmonies arriving on weak beats, and the second of the repeated notes being emphasized over the first — gives the fugue a very subtle off-beat and off-balance feeling.

This fugue has only one subject. In terms of rhythm the subject is monothematic; the entire subject is made up exclusively of eighth notes. Following motivically from its subject, the rest of the fugue is made up predominantly of eighth notes. However, the subject contains two melodic ideas: the first half moves by steps and by jumps, while the second half features repeated notes.

Because rhythms are often easier to hear than all the specific twists and turns in a melody, the exclusive use of eighth notes in this fugue gives the fugue the feeling of being almost monothematic in spite of the fact that the subject does contain two melodic ideas. Bach offsets the potential domination and monotony of eighth notes in this fugue with the most subtle use of syncopation.

What a Life III

Toward the end of his life, Bach went blind. Two operations could not save his eyesight and only worsened his general condition. Because of his increasing blindness, Bach was able to compose less and less in the last few years of his life. On July 28, 1750, Bach died.

As we've seen, Bach is said to have dictated from his deathbed to his son-in-law a chorale prelude on the hymn *Vor deinen Thron tret'*, written for organ. The manuscript for the chorale prelude does not rule out the possibility that it could have been dictated, but neither does it confirm the dictation hypothesis. The manuscript itself offers no conclusive evidence about the manner of composition.

We are now going to look at the music, as opposed to the manuscript of *Vor deinen Thron tret'*, for clues as to whether Bach dictated it on his deathbed. *Vor deinen Thron tret'* is notable musically because it is written in the form of a very interesting fugue. Now that we are almost at the end of the *Well-Tempered,* a closer look at *Vor deinen Thron tret'* will intrigue us.

As we know, a chorale is the hymn sung in the Lutheran church, and a CHORALE PRELUDE is a piece based on the chorale that the organist would play before the chorale itself was sung. A chorale prelude is a very general musical form, its only requirement being that it should be based on the chorale. Often, chorale preludes are simple pieces, little more than ornamentation on the chorale melody and harmony. Sometimes the chorale prelude elaborates on some portion of the chorale tune. Occasionally, a chorale prelude is a long and extensive piece that incorporates, but is not dominated by, the chorale itself. Such is the case with *Vor deinen Thron tret'*. This fugue, written in G Major, has a very sublime feeling.

Vor deinen Thron tret' is a QUADRUPLE FUGUE. That's right, *four* subjects. Bach constructed *Vor deinen Thron tret'* in the following way: he divided the chorale melody into four portions, which serve as the four subjects for the fugue. *Vor deinen Thron tret'* is written for four voices. The lower three voices — alto, tenor, bass — take part in the fugue, while the soprano simply rests when it isn't running a portion of the chorale melody.

The fugue, like the chorale melody, is divided into four sections. Each of the four sections of the fugue begins with an exposition of one of the subjects. After the exposition, each section continues on with more entries of the subject and some measures that don't contain entries. Finally, the subject enters in the soprano in long, slow tones, while the other three voices are continuing on with the fugue. After the conclusion of the entry in the soprano, the fugue moves on to the exposition of the next subject. The second of the three entries in each exposition is the melodic inversion of the subject.

Now, this fugue seems pretty complicated—four subjects, entries in inversion. However, it is really quite simple to follow because Bach never runs entries of different subjects at the same time. We have to follow only one subject at a time. (There are also hints of other subjects from time to time.) In addition, all four subjects move only by step.

The first hint that this piece is Bach's last comes from its title. Typically, chorale preludes are named for the first few words from the first stanza of the chorale hymn. This chorale prelude is not. The first stanza of the hymn for this chorale begins *Wenn wir in höchsten Nöthen sein*, which means "When we are in greatest need." Bach had previously written chorales and chorale preludes titled *Wenn wir in höchsten Nöthen sein*. But this chorale prelude is titled *Vor deinen Thron tret'*, the first words of the second stanza of the hymn. Legend has it that Bach specifically asked for this piece to be titled from the second stanza, not the first. *Vor deinen Thron tret'* means "Before Thy throne I stand."

The second clue that Bach wrote this fugue on his deathbed comes from the soprano part. The first portion of the soprano part contains 14 (=BACH) notes, and the entire part contains 41 (=JSBACH) notes. Bach has made slight changes in the chorale melody in the soprano part apparently to ensure that it has the correct number of notes. Bach certainly used 14's and 41's in other pieces. But it seems he tried doubly hard to get his signature on this piece.

The third clue that Bach dictated this fugue from his deathbed is that this is the only quadruple fugue in all of Bach's compositions. Possibly Bach saved the biggest and best for last.

Despite these clues, it is often argued that this fugue is just too hard for even Bach to have composed solely from memory, without being able to see the piece on the page. To this argument I offer one general and one specific refutation.

In general, I note that, if indeed this is Bach's last composition, he had his whole wonderful life—hundreds of chorales, chorale preludes, fugues, thousands of pieces—on which to draw. Bach was the greatest keyboard player and improvisationalist of his day. It is said that he never saw a piece that he could not sightread on keyboard or organ, and that he was able to improvise three-, four-, five-, even six-voice fugues on the spot. It does not seem inconceivable that such an experienced composer, performer, and improvisationalist could keep one fugue, albeit complex, in his memory while composing it.

You know the old saying, "I have done that so many times I could do it with my eyes closed." Well, consider the end of this fugue. After everything else—the four subjects, the entries in inversion—Bach adds something extra. He runs entries of the fourth subject in stretto, adds an extra voice, and then at the very end of the fugue uses a dramatic chord in minor, even though this fugue is in G Major.

Now let's consider another organ fugue in G Major, the fugue from the Prelude and Fugue for Organ in G Major (BWV 541). At the end of that fugue, what does Bach do? You guessed it: strettos, adds an extra voice, and uses a dramatic chord in minor at the very end. The G Major Organ Fugue was written years before Bach's death.

So Bach had quite literally practiced the end of *Vor deinen Thron tret'* in the G Major Organ Fugue. If Bach did dictate *Vor deinen Thron tret'* on his deathbed, then the end, at least, would not have been so difficult to compose in his head, since he had written something like it already. I'm sure that if we look hard enough, we can find evidence in Bach's other music that he had practiced many other sections of *Vor deinen Thron tret'*.

Here is a final clue that Bach dictated the piece on his deathbed: notice that *Vor deinen Thron tret'* is a chorale prelude written in the form of a fugue. In one piece Bach has managed to represent all of the compositional elements important to him — free-style preludes, structured fugues, and religious devotion. This combination seems like an excellent one for Bach to use in his last piece.

But these clues to show Bach dictated this piece from his deathbed are just that, clues. They don't prove anything. Probably, we will never know whether the legend that Bach dictated *Vor deinen Thron tret'* from his deathbed is true or not. I feel that Bach did, but maybe that's because I want to believe the legend.

b–flat minor
BOOK TWO

THE SUBJECT of b-flat minor Book Two, at four measures, is one of the longer subjects in the *Well-Tempered*. (Only four fugues in the *Well-Tempered* have subjects longer than four measures, though more than ten fugues have four-measure subjects.) This subject also contains many starts and stops as well as a large variety of rhythms — half notes, quarter notes, groups of two eighth notes, and groups of four eighth notes.

You might say that this fugue and g minor Book Two are distantly related members of the same family, this fugue being the slightly older and more serious-sounding relative. Like this fugue, g minor Book Two has a start-and-stop subject. At three measures, however, the subject of g minor Book Two is a little shorter than the subject of this fugue, with a slightly less varied rhythmic content. As with their subjects, this fugue at 101 measures is a little longer than the 84-measure g minor Book Two. G minor Book Two is also the only other fugue in the *Well-Tempered* containing more than one pair of completely overlapping entries (it has three pairs of completely overlapping entries, b-flat minor Book One has one). Overall, g minor Book Two and this fugue have a similar sound and feeling.

To appreciate fully the counterexposition at the end, we have to consider the structure of the rest of the fugue. All 24 entries of this four-voice fugue are contained in the exposition and *five* counterexpositions. Bach has cleverly designed the subject of this fugue to stretto both by complete overlap (in the fifth counterexposition),

LISTENER'S GUIDE
to the b-flat minor Fugue
WELL–TEMPERED CLAVIER
Book Two

PRELUDE

This prelude is dominated by square-sounding, on-the-beat rhythms — eighth notes and quarter notes.

VOICES

4

MAJOR FEATURES

A long, powerful subject.
Counterexpositions.

SPECIAL DEVICES

Counterexpositions (five). This fugue is counterexposition champion along with a minor Book One.

Stretto. This is a fugue that uses stretto.

FORM

First entry in the alto; second entry in the soprano; codetta; third entry in the bass; fourth entry in the tenor; first episode; fifth entry in the tenor, sixth entry in the alto in stretto; seventh entry in the soprano in major, eighth entry in the bass in stretto in minor; second episode; ninth entry in the tenor in inversion; tenth entry in the alto in inversion; two measures; eleventh entry in the soprano in major in inversion; twelfth entry in the bass in minor in inversion; third episode; thirteenth entry in the tenor in inversion, fourteenth entry in the soprano in stretto in inversion; one and a half measures; fifteenth entry in the alto in inversion, sixteenth entry in the bass in stretto in inversion; fourth episode; seventeenth entry in the soprano in major in inversion, eighteenth entry in the tenor in stretto; four and a half measures; nineteenth entry in the bass in minor, twentieth entry in the alto in stretto in inversion; two measures; twenty-first and twenty-second entries simultaneously in the soprano and the alto, twenty-third and twenty-fourth entries in inversion simultaneously in the tenor and the bass — these two entries run in stretto with entries 21 and 22.

---

and after two beats (in the first, third, fourth, and fifth counter-expositions).

Moreover, the subject works in stretto whether the two stretto voices are both running the uninverted, or RECTUS, form of the subject (in the first counterexposition), or both running the inverted form of the subject (in the third counterexposition), or if one voice is running the rectus form of the subject and the other voice is running the inverted form of the subject (in the fourth counterexposition).

Notice how Bach builds the tension in the fugue from (1) the exposition, (2) a counterexposition in stretto, (3) a counterexposition with entries in inversion, (4) a counterexposition in stretto and inversion, (5) a counterexposition in stretto with some entries the rectus version of the subject and others the inverted version of the subject, and (6) the last counterexposition, a counterexposition with two pairs of completely overlapping entries, the pairs of entries running in stretto, the second pair of entries using the melodic inversion of the subject.

Fugues after Bach

What happened to fugues after Bach?

During the last twenty to thirty years of Bach's life, music began to change. The POLY-PHONIC style of the music of Bach and his predecessors, which uses many voices of more or less equal importance, was being replaced by a HOMOPHONIC style, in which one main part is accompanied by the other voices. As the polyphonic style disappeared, so too did fugues, which by their very nature are polyphonic.

So great was the respect for fugues and the reputation of the fugue as a compositional tour de force, however, that they did not vanish completely.

Two main types of fugues were written after Bach. The first type, ACADEMIC FUGUES, have been written by lesser composers and music theorists. The trouble with academic fugues is that they are composed under the belief that fugues must adhere to a large set of technical and complex rules. For example, it was thought that a fugue should have a certain amount of stretto, beginning at a certain place in the fugue, and a certain number of entries and a counterexposition at a preassigned spot in the fugue. Adherence to all these rules can make academic fugues sound dry, complicated, stiff, and boring. In contrast to the many rules of academic fugues, Bach used only a handful of general rules when writing his fugues. Within those few rules he exercised immense creativity and flexibility.

The second type of fugue written after Bach consists of a small number of FUGUES WRITTEN BY THE GREAT MASTERS, such as Beethoven's *Grosse Fuge* and the "Kyrie" from Mozart's *Requiem*. These fugues are usually wonderful pieces, but even with fugues written by the masters there are dangers. No matter how good a composer is, if the composer writes only a couple of fugues, there is a natural tendency to try to throw everything into them, making them excessively long and complex.

I think the best fugue written since Bach's time is the fugue in the *Variations and Fugue on a Theme by Handel* (Op. 24, 1861), by Johannes Brahms.

B Major

BOOK TWO

WHEN I hear B Major Book Two I really get the feeling that the *Well-Tempered* is almost over. This is the last in a series of four long and very serious-sounding fugues — a minor, B-flat Major, b-flat minor, and this fugue — before the more playful b minor Book Two that concludes the *Well-Tempered*.

This fugue is also the last of the three OLD-STYLE FUGUES in Book Two. Like E-flat Major Book Two and E Major Book Two, this one has many features of fugues written in times before Bach's: a very singable subject, a lowest to highest — bass to soprano — order of entries, a $\frac{2}{2}$ time signature, and an abundance of long notes. And, like the other old-style fugues in Book Two, this one uses a large-level special device: it is a double fugue.

This fugue is a curious cross between the two types of double fugues — the type in which the subjects are exposed separately, and the type in which the two subjects are exposed together, the second subject accompanying all entries of the first. The second subject in this fugue doesn't enter until the sixth entry of the first subject. From then on, however, the second subject accompanies eight of the remaining nine entries of the first subject, with only two entries of the second that are not accompanying an entry of the first.

Also like the other old-style fugues in Book Two, this one contains a feature of newer (for Bach) styles: the second subject uses faster notes compared with the slower, old-style notes of the first subject.

LISTENER'S GUIDE
to the B Major Fugue
WELL–TEMPERED CLAVIER
Book Two

PRELUDE

I like the solo runs in the middle of this prelude.

VOICES

4

MAJOR FEATURE AND SPECIAL DEVICE

Double fugue.

FORM

First entry of the first subject in the bass; second entry of the first subject in the tenor; codetta; third entry of the first subject in the alto; fourth entry of the first subject in the soprano; one measure; fifth entry of the first subject in the bass; first episode; sixth entry of the first subject in the tenor, first entry of the second subject in the soprano; second entry of the second subject in the tenor; third entry of the second subject in the soprano; seventh entry of the first subject in the alto, fourth entry of the second subject in the bass; second episode; eighth entry of the first subject in the soprano, fifth entry of the second subject in the alto; third episode; ninth entry of the first subject in the bass in minor, sixth entry of the second subject in the soprano; one measure; tenth entry of the first subject in the tenor in major, seventh entry of the second subject in the alto; fourth episode; eleventh entry of the first subject in the tenor in minor, eighth entry of the second subject in the soprano; fifth episode (long); twelfth entry of the first subject in the bass in major; sixth episode; thirteenth entry of the first subject in the alto, ninth entry of the second subject in the alto; tenth entry of the second subject in the bass; two measures; fourteenth and last entry of the first subject in the soprano, eleventh and last entry of the second subject in the tenor; coda.

LISTENING HINT

The fifth episode is very long.

Thirty-four of the 38 single fugues in the *Well-Tempered* have two or more motivic ideas contained in their subject, and Bach employs one of two schemes to ensure that this is so in the ten double and triple fugues in the *Well-Tempered:* (1) At least one of the two or three individual subjects contains at least two motivic ideas, or (2) all the individual subjects are monothematic, but with radically different themes from each other. So between them, the subjects contain more than one idea.

B Major Book Two is an excellent example of the second scheme. Both subjects are monothematic: the first subject uses slow notes and jumps, and the second uses fast notes and steps. Between them, the two subjects furnish this fugue with two motivic ideas.

b minor
BOOK TWO

SO WE have come to the end of the *Well-Tempered Clavier.* Twenty-four preludes and fugues in Book One, 23 preludes and fugues in Book Two. Now we have arrived at b minor Book Two, the last fugue in Book Two, the last fugue in the *Well-Tempered Clavier.* How does Bach end Book Two of the *Well-Tempered?*

To end Book One, as we have seen, Bach used a very clever device. For the final fugue in Book One, b minor, Bach employed a subject containing all 12 chromatic notes. What better way, apparently, to end the first book of the *Well-Tempered Clavier* — a collection of pieces consisting of a prelude and fugue in *every* key — than with a fugue whose subject contains *every* chromatic note?

The only difficulty is that a subject with all the chromatic notes must be very slow. If it were not, the audience would not be able to adjust to all the chromatic notes and the changing chords accompanying the chromatic notes, and the subject would just sound silly. But a slow subject means a slow fugue, and b minor Book One is very, very slow. B minor Book One is also very long, one of the two or three longest in the *Well-Tempered* in terms of performance time, the length being necessary to work through all the melodic and harmonic implications of the chromatic notes. So, while a subject containing all the chromatic notes is a clever and interesting idea for the last fugue in Book One, the consequences of such a subject—a very long and slow fugue — may not make for the best way to end a book of the *Well-Tempered Clavier.*

LISTENER'S GUIDE
to the b minor Fugue
WELL–TEMPERED CLAVIER
Book Two

PRELUDE

This prelude has a feeling of finality.

VOICES

3

MAJOR FEATURE

Bittersweet subject.

FORM

First entry in the alto; second entry in the soprano; codetta; third entry in the bass; first episode; fourth entry in the alto; second episode; fifth entry in the soprano in major; third episode; sixth entry in the bass in major; fourth episode; seventh entry in the alto in minor; fifth episode; eighth entry in the bass in minor; sixth episode; ninth and last entry in the *Well-Tempered* in the soprano; coda.

LISTENING HINTS

1. The first, second, and third episodes are very short. The fifth episode is long.

2. The coda is very long and contains a fake entry of the subject.

To end Book Two, Bach tried a different approach. For the subject of b minor Book Two, he concentrated more on the feeling of the subject than on the technical form of the subject, as he did for b minor Book One. From the outset, b minor Book Two has a bittersweet and final, yet also forward-looking, feeling. To imbue the fugue with these feelings Bach uses a subject that is fast, but not too fast, and sad, but also somewhat hopeful-sounding.

Consciously, I think, Bach begins the subject of this fugue with the same three notes descending in a chordal pattern with which he began the subject of b minor Book One. But after that subjects of b minor Book One and b minor Book Two are quite different.

Notice that in the subject of this fugue, Bach twice uses a three-note pattern consisting of a pitch, the same pitch an OCTAVE (eight steps) lower, and then the original pitch. Octave jumps were not very common in the melodies of Bach's pieces, but they became much more common in music written after Bach.

To make this final fugue in the *Well-Tempered Clavier* easy for the audience to follow, Bach uses a very simple overall structure: the entries in the middle section of this fugue alternate strictly with the episodes. That is, between every two entries (in the middle section) there is an episode, and between every two episodes there is an entry. The strict alternation and the easy-to-hear subject make this a simple fugue, one in which the distinction between the episodes and entries is utterly clear.

Bach adds one last powerful touch to this fugue — a move to major. (Maybe it's just me, but from its very beginning, I can just feel that this fugue is going to do that.) The oh so wonderful and happy move to major arrives with the fifth and sixth entries in major. The fugue returns to minor and finishes with three more entries in minor, three more episodes, and the coda.

Thus concludes the *Well-Tempered Clavier.*

The WELL–TEMPERED in Review

The story is told of a man who came to two great rabbis and asked them to tell him all the wisdom in the Bible while he stood on one leg.

One rabbi sent the man away, saying that there was much too much to know in the Bible to learn while standing on one leg. But the other rabbi said to the man, "Love your neighbor as yourself. The rest is commentary. Now go and learn."

Similarly, we can say, "The subject is the star of a fugue. The rest is commentary. Now go and listen."

PART FOUR

APPENDIXES

MORE ON STRETTO

MISCONCEPTIONS AND TRUTHS ABOUT STRETTO

Misconceptions

1. Stretto is a device used rarely by Bach, and only in special situations.

2. A fugue starts strettoing near its *end* and intensifies the stretto as the fugue progresses further toward its end.

3. During the stretto, voices jump in all over the place on top of each other, making for a rousing conclusion to the fugue.

Truths

1. Stretto is not rare in the *Well-Tempered;* Bach used it a lot, in twenty of the 48 fugues in the *Well-Tempered.* Stretto is one of the most common large-level devices in the *Well-Tempered.* A chart of the fugues in the *Well-Tempered* with stretto in them is in "Stretto Fugues and Fugues That Use Stretto."

2. Fugues are much more likely to start strettoing in the *first* half of the fugue than near the end. Twelve of the 20 fugues with stretto in the *Well-Tempered* (60 percent) start strettoing in the first half.

Where Fugues from the *Well-Tempered* Having Stretto in Them Start Strettoing

50% or Earlier	51%–75%	Later than 80%
BOOK ONE		
C Major (26%)	G Major (60%)	
d minor (32%)	b-flat minor (67%)	
d-sharp minor (31%)	B Major (62%)	
F Major (38%)		
g minor (50%)		
a minor (32%)		
BOOK TWO		
c minor (50%)	d minor (63%)	f minor (87%)
C-sharp Major (26%)	d-sharp minor (54%)	A-flat Major (84%)
D Major (28%)	g minor (54%)	
E-flat Major (44%)		
E Major (21%)		
b-flat minor (27%)		

Fugues are actually just as likely to *abate* their stretto at the end of a fugue, or *never intensify the stretto at all,* than to intensify the stretto at the end of the fugue, as shown in the next chart.

Where Fugues from the *Well-Tempered* with Stretto in Them Start Intensifying the Stretto

Never, or Abated before Two-Thirds Mark	Earlier than 80%	Later than 80%
BOOK ONE		
C Major	d-sharp minor	G Major
d minor	a minor	g minor
F Major		b-flat minor
B Major		
BOOK TWO		
C-sharp Major	c minor	d-sharp minor
d minor	D Major	E Major
E-flat Major		b-flat minor
f minor		
g minor		
A-flat Major		

3. Bach did not use stretto in only one way — all the voices piling on top of each other at the end of a fugue — but in many, many different ways.

Bach's uses of stretto range from the Great Stretto Fugue, C Major Book One, in which stretto appears everywhere in the fugue, finally abating at the end of the fugue; to E-flat Major Book Two with its three pairs of stretto entries of that fugue's wonderful singing subject scattered throughout the fugue; to E Major Book Two and its counterexpositions in stretto; to b-flat minor Book One, which does indeed increase its stretto as the fugue progresses; to f minor Book Two, a fugue that hardly uses stretto at all, which has just a single pair of stretto entries overlapping by only three notes.

Bach did not write fugues to show off stretto, but rather used stretto to help write great fugues.

UPSIDE DOWN AND
CHANGE OF PACE

USUALLY, TO build sections of a fugue from the subject, Bach will use FRAGMENTATION AND SEQUENCE. Bach will build a section of a fugue by using a fragment of the subject and run that fragment in sequence, two, three, or more times. Fragmentation and sequence is a tried-and-true technique that Bach uses successfully over and over and over again in his fugues.

Occasionally, Bach wants to introduce some more variety than can be gotten by fragmentation and sequence (but still keep his fugues motivic). In these cases Bach will often use melodic inversion, augmentation, or diminution.

To invert means to turn upside down. The MELODIC INVERSION of the subject of a fugue is literally the subject turned upside down. When a subject goes up, the subject's inversion goes down. When a subject goes down, its inversion goes up.

The AUGMENTATION of the subject of a fugue is the original subject with all the notes increased proportionately by the same amount. Typically, when a composer uses the augmentation of the subject of a fugue, the composer will double the lengths of all the notes in the original subject. Unlike the melodic inversion of a subject, which changes the direction of a subject, the augmentation of a subject does not alter its internal fabric. The augmentation changes nothing about the subject — its direction, the relative lengths of its notes, etc. — except the absolute lengths of the notes.

The DIMINUTION of the subject of a fugue is the original subject with all the notes decreased proportionately by the same amount. Usually, when composers use the diminution of the subject of a fugue, they will cut the lengths of all the notes in the original subject in half. If the original subject uses half notes and eighth notes, the diminution of the subject will use quarter notes and sixteenth notes. Like the augmentation of the subject of a fugue, the diminution of the subject changes nothing about the subject except the absolute lengths of the notes.

Listed here are the fugues in the *Well-Tempered* that use the melodic inversion, augmentation, or diminution of their subject.

Inversion, Augmentation, and Diminution in the *Well-Tempered*

Book One	Book Two
INVERSION	
c-sharp minor (second subject)	c minor
d minor	C-sharp Major
d-sharp minor	c-sharp minor (first subject)
F-sharp Major (second subject)	d minor
f-sharp minor (first subject)	d-sharp minor
G Major	f-sharp minor (third subject)
a minor	b-flat minor
B Major	
AUGMENTATION	
d-sharp minor	c minor
	C-sharp Major
DIMINUTION	
	C-sharp Major
	E Major

NOTES:

1. Fifteen fugues in the *Well-Tempered* use the melodic inversion of the subject. Only three use the augmentation of the subject. Only two use the diminution of the subject.

2. D sharp minor Book One, c minor Book Two, and C-sharp Major Book Two have entries of the melodic inversion of the subject and also entries of the augmentation of the subject.

3. C-sharp Major Book Two has entries of the melodic inversion of the subject, entries of the augmentation of the subject, and entries of the diminution of the subject. C-sharp Major Book Two even has entries of the subject both in inversion *and* diminution.

We are so accustomed to listening for the original version of the subject that it is very difficult to hear the inversion, which moves in the opposite direction. So it comes as a bit of a surprise to me to see that there are so many entries of the subject in inversion in the *Well-Tempered*.

But although it is hard to hear, the inversion of the subject is a useful tool for introducing variety into a piece, while at the same time maintaining its motivicness. The inversion of the subject of a fugue preserves two important characteristics of the original version — the rhythm and the overall shape (turned upside down, of course). When we hear an entry of the inversion of the subject, we might not be able to recognize it as the subject. Nevertheless, we will probably be able to recognize many aspects of the rhythm and overall shape of the original version.

The augmentation and diminution of the subject are even harder to hear than the inversion. An entry of the augmentation of the subject takes so long that we in the audience might well get distracted and start following something else before the entry of the augmentation of the subject is over.

OTHER FUGUES

THE 48 fugues in the *Well-Tempered* do not exist in a vacuum. Bach wrote hundreds of other fugues — fugues for harpsichord and for organ, fugues for instruments other than keyboard instruments, and fugues for singers.

Often, study of the other fugues confirms trends we have seen in the *Well-Tempered* — for example, trends concerning the predominance of the subject of a fugue, the frequency of stretto and double and triple fugues, and the use of stretto at the beginning, not the end, of a fugue. Sometimes study of other fugues enhances and enlarges our knowledge about fugues derived from the *Well-Tempered* — for example, other fugues clarify what types of musical phrases make good fugue subjects.

Occasionally, other fugues exemplify trends and ideas not seen at all in the *Well-Tempered*. For example, in the *Well-Tempered* the middle section is almost always by far the longest section in a fugue, while in some other fugues the exposition or coda is the longest section.

The other fugues are also great pieces. Some rank among the best of all Bach's compositions, fugues or not. In this essay I list some other fugues in Bach's compositions and some of my other favorites. In the next essay I discuss Bach's organ fugues — close cousins of fugues in the *Well-Tempered* — in a bit more depth.

Besides the *Well-Tempered* Bach wrote many fugues for harpsichord and other keyboard instruments. Some of these harpsichord fugues, such as the Chromatic Fantasy and Fugue (BWV 903), are not part of any collection. Others can be found amidst Bach's many harpsichord compositions — for example, the last section of the D Major Toccata for harpsichord (BWV 912) is a fugue. There are also undoubtedly hundreds of fugues that Bach improvised on the harpsichord and never wrote down.

See the next essay for details on Bach's many organ fugues. Alas, as with the harpsichord fugues, Bach must have improvised countless fugues on the organ that he never wrote down and are lost forever.

Bach's many fugues for various instruments and combinations of instruments range from fugues for a solo violin or cello, to a fugue for flute, violin, and cello, to fugues in the Brandenburg Concertos scored for an entire orchestra. It is truly remarkable that Bach was able to write a solo fugue — a fugue for only one instrument — since a solo fugue is akin to a one-person crowd.

Bach's cantatas and other vocal works, such as the B Minor Mass, contain more than 100 fugues for various combinations of singers and singers with instruments. Along with the instrumental fugues, Bach's vocal fugues are among his best and most inspirational pieces.

The *Musical Offering* and the *Art of the Fugue* are two collections of pieces Bach wrote in the last few years of his life. The *Musical Offering* contains two fugues, ten canons, and a trio sonata based on a theme of Frederick the Great. The *Art of the Fugue* contains fourteen fugues and four canons based on a theme composed by Bach.

Some Favorite Other Fugues

	BWV	*Instrumentation*
Brandenburg Concerto No. 2, third movement	1046	trumpet, flute, oboe, solo violin, strings, continuo
Cantata 50, *Nun ist das Heil*	50	two choruses (8 voices), 3 trumpets, timpani, 3 oboes, strings, continuo
Sonata for Solo Violin in C Major, second movement	1005	solo violin
Sonata for Solo Violin in g minor, second movement	1001	solo violin
Magnificat, eleventh movement, "Sicut locutus est"	243	5 voices, continuo
Toccata for Harpsichord in D Major, last section	912	harpsichord
Sonata for Viola da Gamba in G Major, fourth movement	1027	viola da gamba, harpsichord
Suite for Solo Cello in c minor, first movement	1011	solo cello
Goldberg Variations, tenth variation	988	harpsichord

ORGAN FUGUES

ORGAN FUGUES are close cousins of fugues written for the harpsichord. As we enjoy the wonderful organ fugues, they can be helpful to us in learning about and enjoying fugues from the *Well-Tempered*.

In "Preludes I" we said that for the sake of temporal balance it was important for a fugue to have some kind of preluding material. All but one of Bach's organ fugues have some kind of preluding material to achieve temporal balance with the fugue. Most of Bach's organ fugues are part of prelude and fugue pairs. The word *prelude* in the context of a prelude and fugue for organ means simply "any music that comes before a fugue." Some of Bach's other organ fugues have more specific preluding material such as a TOCCATA — a free-flowing North German–style piece that usually featured arpeggios and improvisatory runs — or a PASSACAGLIA — a more strict contrapuntal form featuring a four-measure or eight-measure repeating phrase in the bass.

In the first chart most of Bach's major organ fugues are listed. The fugues are listed by their preluding material. Nicknames for the fugues, most of which have come about since Bach's time, are in parentheses.

Key	BWV
PRELUDES AND FUGUES	
C Major	531
D Major	532
f minor	534
g minor	535
A Major	536
d minor	539
G Major ("Great")	541
a minor ("Great")	543
b minor	544
C Major	545
c minor	546
C Major	547
e minor ("Wedge")	548
c minor	549
G Major	550
TOCCATAS AND FUGUES	
d minor ("Dorian")	538
F Major	540
d minor ("Great")	565
FANTASIES AND FUGUES	
c minor	537
g minor ("Great")	542
c minor	562
OTHER ORGAN FUGUES	
Toccata, Adagio, and Fugue in C Major	564
Fugue in g minor ("Little")	578
Passacaglia and Fugue in c minor	582

NOTES:

1. Many fugues have the nickname "Great." There is one in G Major (BWV 541), one in a minor (BWV 543), one in d minor (BWV 565), and one in g minor (BWV 542).

2. The d minor Toccata and Fugue BWV 565 should be familiar to anyone who has seen a horror movie.

3. The fugue from the Fantasia and Fugue in c minor (BWV 562) was left incomplete by Bach.

4. The "Little" g minor fugue (BWV 578) has no preluding material.

5. Except for the Prelude and Fugue in f minor (which has four flats) none of the organ fugues is written for keys with more than three sharps or flats.

SPECIAL DEVICES IN BACH'S ORGAN FUGUES

Organ Fugues with Stretto in Them

Key	BWV	What Percent of the Way Through?	How Much Stretto?
f minor	534	89	Fugue That Hardly Uses Stretto at All
A Major	536	75	Fugue That Hardly Uses Stretto at All
d minor	538	45	Fugue That Uses Stretto
G Major	541	87	Fugue That Uses Stretto
C Major	547	49	Fugue That Uses Stretto
c minor	562	[See Note #1]	Stretto Fugue

NOTES:

1. Bach left the fugue from the Fantasia and Fugue in c minor (BWV 562) incomplete. It clearly was going to be a stretto fugue: it starts strettoing only seven measures after the end of its exposition.

2. As with the fugues from the *Well-Tempered*, organ fugues often start strettoing in their first half.

Organ Fugues That Are Double Fugues

Key	BWV
c minor	537
F Major	540
c minor	546
e minor	548
c minor	582

A TOP SIX AND A TOP FOUR

(listed by ascending BWV number, not in order of preference)

Top Six Organ Fugues

Key	BWV
g minor	535
G Major	541
g minor	542
C Major	564
d minor	565
g minor	578

Top Four Preluding Material

Key	BWV
Toccata in F Major	540
Toccata and Adagio in C Major	564
Toccata in d minor	565
Passacaglia in c minor	582

THE C MAJOR TWO–PART
INVENTION

IN "WHAT IS A FUGUE?" we said that the word FUGUE comes from the Latin verb *fugo*, meaning flee, chase, or follow. We noted that in music the word *follow* often means imitate. Fugues were originally pieces in which the various voices imitated each other. As a result of a few hundred years of development and change between the first fugues and Bach's time, the imitating nature of fugues was largely lost. However, some aspects of their imitating heritage remain even in Bach's fugues; for example, in the exposition of a Bach fugue each voice in turn has the subject of the fugue exactly once.

Besides fugues there are many other genres of IMITATIVE PIECES. One such genre we have discussed in the *Essential Listener's Guide* is the canon. Canons have much more imitation than fugues.

Here we discuss yet another genre of imitative piece, the invention, and one invention in particular, the C Major Two-Part Invention.

As a genre of imitative pieces, INVENTIONS are close cousins of fugues. Like fugues, inventions have three sections — exposition, middle section, and coda. In the exposition, each voice has the theme of the invention exactly once. We call the theme of an invention the MOTIVE of the invention. (The word *subject* is reserved for the theme of a fugue.) Though similar to fugues, inventions are simpler. The relative simplicity of inventions compared with fugues derives from the following:

In a fugue the second voice to enter has the subject five notes higher than the first entry. (The third entry of the subject comes in on the same note as the first entry. If there is a fourth entry, then the fourth entry, like the second entry, comes in five steps higher than the first entry. For more on this feature of fugues see "Real and Tonal Answers" accompanying E-flat Major Book Two.) In an invention the second entry of the motive (and third voice if there is one) comes in on the same note as the first entry.

In music there is a natural tension between a given note and the note five steps higher. So a fugue has much more built-in tension than an invention, and thus can be longer and more complicated without getting boring.

It turns out that inventions have less rigorously designed middle sections than fugues and do not have the sharp progression between entries of the motive and episodes of a fugue.

The C Major Two-Part Invention has one of the simplest motives of all the inventions. It is the first in a collection of Two-Part Inventions by Bach and it seems that he has deliberately used an extremely simple theme to show that even so he can write a wonderful piece. Recall that the first fugue in Book One of the *Well-Tempered,* C Major, also has a very simple subject.

The C Major Invention is so easy to play that it is often assigned to beginning piano students. But despite its simple theme, and despite the fact that so many piano students perform it, the C Major Invention never gets boring or worn out.

Why? The answer, both in the specific and the general, is motivicness. This invention contains 47 entries of the motive, which often run against each other in a very interesting way. With all the entries of the motive running against each other, no matter how many times you listen to this piece you feel as if you have missed some of the entries, because you really have, and you want to hear the piece again. Of course, the next time you hear the piece you'll miss something so you'll want to hear the piece again. And so on.

Bach runs the motive of this invention against itself in an interesting, almost miraculous way. The motive of this invention is only two beats long. The first beat of the motive goes up by step, and the second beat goes down in a jumping pattern. In this invention Bach uses both the melodic inversion and the retrograde of the motive. RETROGRADE, which comes from the Latin *retro,* back, and *gradus,* step, means the motive runs backward. Just so I can convince you that the retrograde of a theme is different from the inversion of a theme, I give the motive of this invention, the inversion of the motive, and the retrograde of the motive (facing page).

This invention is one of the precious few of Bach's pieces that use the retrograde of a theme. (The "Crab" Canon from the *Musical Offering* is another.) The reason Bach uses the retrograde of a theme so rarely is that it is exceedingly difficult for the audience to hear a theme run backward.

Other microscale special devices, such as inversion, augmentation, and diminution, are much, much easier to hear than the retrograde. For example, the inversion of a theme preserves the relative and absolute lengths of notes in a theme, as well as its shape. (Of course, the inversion of a theme turns the theme upside down.) The augmentation and diminution of a theme preserve everything about a theme—its shape, its direction of motion, and the relative proportion of notes—except the absolute length of all the notes. But the retrograde preserves nothing about the theme. The only way to hear it is to remember the whole theme and then think of how that theme would sound backward, all the while listening to a piece that keeps moving on.

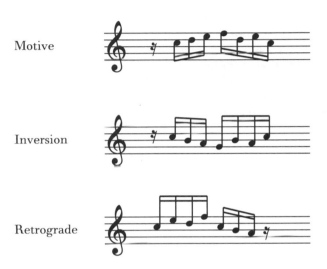

The only reason the retrograde works in this piece is that the theme is so short, only two beats, and the two beats are so distinct that while listening to the piece it is possible to notice how the theme sounds running backward.

Bach uses the retrograde of the motive in the following way: In the soprano part toward the beginning of the piece, and then in the bass part a little later, Bach runs the melodic inversion of the theme over and over again in sequence. However, instead of just the two-beat motive running over and over again, because of the special design of the motive we have the following situation. Consider the inversion of the motive run twice in a row:

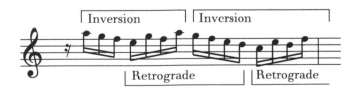

The first two beats above are the inversion of the motive. But overlapping with the first two beats, the second and third beats are the retrograde of the theme. So how do we hear the third beat above? As the second beat of an entry of the inversion of the subject? Or as the first beat of an entry of the retrograde of the subject? If we hear the third beat as the inversion, then we miss the retrograde. If we hear the third beat as the retrograde, then we miss the inversion.

Bach uses sequences similiar to the above many times in this invention. Because of ambiguous beats, like the third beat above, no matter how many times we hear the invention we will always miss something, so we will want to hear it again, and again, and again. It is amazing that Bach has been able to design a piece so that every time we hear it, we miss part of it. This trick of the ambiguous beats is one of the most miraculous in all Bach's music. Bach uses a similar trick of ambiguous beats in E-flat Major Book Two. See the essay on that fugue for details.

THE BACH OF LISTS

Number of Entries of the Subject per Fugue in the *Well-Tempered**

Number of entries	6	8	9	10	11	12	14	15	16	17	18	22	23	24	27	29	37	44
Number of fugues	1	6	5	5	5	4	4	2	4	1	1	1	1	4	1	1	1	1

As we can see, Bach used many entries of the subject in his fugues. All the fugues from the *Well-Tempered* have at least eight entries, except G Major Book Two, which has six. The median number of entries for fugues from the *Well-Tempered* is 12. That is, half of the fugues in the *Well-Tempered* have 12 or fewer entries of the subject, and half have 12 or more entries of the subject.

Percentage of Fugues from the *Well-Tempered* Taken Up by Their (First) Subject**

Percent	30–35	36–40	41–45	46–50	51–55	56–60	61–65	66–70	71–75	76–80	86–90
Number of fugues	5	2	7	7	6	7	4	4	4	1	1

As we can see, entries of the subject occupy a very large percentage of almost all fugues in the *Well-Tempered.* The median percent occupancy of

*In double and triple fugues I count the entries of the first subject only.

**For double and triple fugues I list the percentage of the fugue occupied by entries of the first subject only.

fugues from the *Well-Tempered* by their subject is between 51 and 55: more than half the fugues in the *Well-Tempered* are more than half filled by entries of their subject.

Notice that just as none of the fugues in the *Well-Tempered* is less than 30 percent occupied by entries of its subject, few are more than 70 percent occupied by entries of their subject. Excessive entries of the subject dilute its power and effectiveness.

Orders of Entries and the Number of Fugues from the *Well-Tempered* That Use Them

	Book One	Book Two	Well-Tempered Total
TWO-VOICE FUGUE			
S, B	1	0	1
THREE-VOICE FUGUES			
S, A, B	7	6	13
A, S, B	4	5	9
B, S, A	0	2	2
B, A, S	0	2	2
			26
FOUR-VOICE FUGUES			
T, A, S, B	2	2	4
B, T, A, S	1	3	4
A, S, T, B	1	2	3
A, S, B, T	2	1	3
A, T, B, S	1	1	2
T, A, B, S	2	0	2
T, B, S, A	1	0	1
			19
FIVE-VOICE FUGUES			
SI, SII, A, T, B	1	0	1
B, T, A, SI, SII	1	0	1
			2
TOTALS	24	24	48

KEY:
S–soprano, A–alto, T–tenor, B–bass.
For five-voice fugues, from highest to lowest: SI–soprano I, SII–soprano II, A-alto, T-tenor, B-bass.

NOTES:
1. All the fugues in Book Two are either three- or four-voice fugues.

2. Twenty-six of the 48 fugues in the *Well-Tempered* are three-voice fugues.

3. Twenty-two of the 26 three-voice fugues have their last entry in the bass, while only seven of the 19 four-voice fugues have their last entry in the bass.

4. The two five-voice fugues have either a highest to lowest — soprano I to bass — or lowest to highest — bass to soprano I — order of entries. Bach probably used these orders of entry in the five-voice fugues to make these fugues, with more voices than all the other fugues in the *Well-Tempered*, easier to follow.

Time Signatures of Preludes and Fugues in the *Well-Tempered*

	Book One			Book Two			Well-Tempered
	Preludes	Fugues	Total	Preludes	Fugues	Total	Total
$\frac{2}{4}$	0	0	0	1	2	3	3
$\frac{3}{4}$	1	3	4	6	2	8	14
$\frac{4}{4}$	14	16	30	8	8	16	46
$\frac{6}{4}$	1	1	2	0	0	0	2
$\frac{2}{2}$	0	1	1	3	6	9	10
$\frac{5}{2}$	1	0	1	1	1	2	3
$\frac{3}{8}$	1	1	2	2	2	4	6
$\frac{6}{8}$	1	1	2	0	1	1	3
$\frac{9}{8}$	1	1	2	2	0	2	4
$\frac{12}{8}$	2	0	2	1	0	1	3
$\frac{6}{16}$	0	0	0	0	1	1	1
$\frac{12}{16}$	1	0	1	1	1	2	3
$\frac{24}{16}$	1	0	1	0	0	0	1
TOTALS	24	24	48	25*	24	49*	97*

NOTE:

Forty-six out of the 96 pieces in the *Well-Tempered*, 30 out of the 48 pieces in Book One alone, are written in $\frac{4}{4}$.

*The C-sharp Major prelude Book Two is written in two parts, the first part in $\frac{4}{4}$, the second part in $\frac{3}{8}$.

TOP TENS

IN THESE lists, preludes and fugues are listed in their order of appearance in the *Well-Tempered Clavier*.

MY TOP TEN PRELUDES

Book One

C Major
c minor
C-sharp Major
E-flat Major
F-sharp Major
g minor
g-sharp minor

Book Two

C Major
F-sharp Major
G Major

MY TOP TEN SUBJECTS

Book One

c minor
C-sharp Major
F-sharp Major (first subject)

G Major
B-flat Major

Book Two

C Major
E-flat Major
F Major
f minor
a minor (combination of both subjects)

MY TOP TEN EPISODES

Book One

c minor, first episode
c minor, fourth episode
C-sharp Major, fifth episode
F-sharp Major, fourth episode
G Major, first, second, third, and fifth
    episodes (a four-way tie!)

Book Two

C Major, first episode
C Major, fourth episode
F Major, second episode
f minor, first episode
a minor, first episode

THE TOP TEN FUGUES

THE SUPERSTAR FOUR

c minor Book One
F-sharp Major Book One
C Major Book Two
E-flat Major Book Two

The Other Greats

C Major Book One
C-sharp Major Book One
g minor Book One
B-flat Major Book One
f minor Book Two
a minor Book Two

INDEX

Page numbers in **boldface** type refer to the main entry for each fugue.